against the stream

against the stream

Christianity and mission in an age of globalization

David W. Smith

Inter-Varsity Press

INTER-VARSITY PRESS
38 De Montfort Street, Leicester LE1 7GP, England
Email: ivp@uccf.org.uk
Website: www.ivpbooks.com

British Library Cataloguing in Publication Data
A catalogue record for this book is available from the British Library.

ISBN 0–85111–793–7

Set in Monotype Dante 10.5 / 13pt

Typeset in Great Britain by Servis Filmsetting Ltd, Manchester
Printed and bound in Great Britain by CPD Wales, Ebbw Vale

*Inter-Varsity Press is the publishing division of the Universities and
Colleges Christian Fellowship (formerly the Inter-Varsity Fellowship), a
student movement linking Christian Unions in universities and colleges
throughout Great Britain, and a member movement of the International
Fellowship of Evangelical Students. For more information about local
and national activities write to UCCF, 38 De Montfort Street, Leicester
LE1 7GP, email us at email@uccf.org.uk, or visit the UCCF website at
www.uccf.org.uk.*

Contents

Introduction

In September 2001 I found myself in Northern Nigeria in the immediate aftermath of the destruction of the Twin Towers in New York which had occurred a matter of days earlier. Prior to my arrival in Jos – and weeks before the events in America – there had been an outbreak of very serious inter-communal and inter-religious violence in Plateau State which resulted in great loss of life. At the time of my departure for Abuja the British Foreign Office was warning travellers to suspend plans to go to Nigeria. However, I was anxious to return to the Theological College of Northern Nigeria at Bukuru in order to lecture as had been agreed some time earlier and I discovered that teaching in such a context was, as may be imagined, a challenging and enlightening experience.

Not surprisingly, passions were running high on both sides of the divide between Christian and Muslim communities. The attack on the United States seemed only to confirm the suspicions of many Christians in Nigeria that Islam remained an essentially backward, reactive and inherently violent religion, unable to come to terms with the flow of history and the global spread of modernity. When pictures of Osama bin Laden began to appear in the windows of taxis driven by Muslims in Jos and it became known that newborn sons within the Muslim community were being named 'Osama', after the man responsible for the terrorist assault on the West, these fears appeared to be confirmed.

This was the context within which the material contained in chapter 4 of this book came to birth. I must express my gratitude to the staff and students at TCNN both for their generous hospitality at that time and for giving me the privilege of delivering the lecture on which this chapter is based. I salute these colleagues whose commitment to discovering the way of Christ in a context characterized by deep religious and ethnic divisions is a shining example of what it really means to do Christian theology in the cutting-edge situations of a pluralist world today. This lecture was subsequently published both in the *TCNN Research Bulletin* in Nigeria and, in an edited form, in the journal *Themelios* and I am grateful to the editors of both publications for their help and encouragement.

The themes found in that chapter, dealing with Christianity and modernity, and with the theological and missiological issues arising in a religiously pluralist context, will be discovered recurring in different ways throughout this book. The collection of lectures and essays here gathered together are *Against the Stream* both in the sense that they argue that Christian theology and mission are inevitably countercultural in a globalized world that is being shaped by materialist and economic values, and in that they challenge certain received, stereotyped patterns of understanding within the Christian community with regard to our response to this world.

At the same time, I must correct any misunderstanding that might arise from the title of this book: I am far from wishing to argue that the appropriate Christian position in the face of globalization is a merely negative one involving only resistance and opposition to the world. On the contrary, as I hope becomes clear in the final chapter, I want to affirm the fact that this is a great time to be alive since the church of Christ now looks more like the numberless, multi-ethnic crowd seen in John's vision in the book of Revelation than at any previous point in history. We have good grounds to hope that the ancient prophetic

promise of the final blessing of all nations is closer to fulfilment than
ever before. Nonetheless, if we are really to grasp the significance of
this, there is an urgent need, particularly within Western Christianity,
for a renewed and fresh vision which will create openness to new perspectives in mission and theology. My hope and prayer is that the
chapters that follow might make some contribution toward such a refocusing on the missionary calling of the whole people of God.

With the exception of chapter 7, the material contained in this book
originated in various lectures given over the past few years. I have
tried to eliminate overlap as much as possible but doubtless some evidence of this still remains in what follows. I am grateful to the Council
of the Keswick Convention, and especially to its chairman, Peter
Maiden, for the invitations to deliver lectures at the convention from
which chapters 1 and 2 are derived, and for the encouraging and stimulating feedback I obtained to these presentations. The material in
chapter 1 also formed the basis for the Catherwood Lecture delivered at
the invitation of the Evangelical Coalition of Northern Ireland in Belfast
in 2002. I was delighted to be thus associated with the work of ECONI,
which has long seemed to me to provide a model of theology and ethics
that are both faithful and contextual.

Chapter 3 was prepared as a lecture for the Edinburgh Dogmatics
Conference in 2001, held at the Free Church College, and I am grateful
to the then-Warden of Rutherford House, Edinburgh, David Searle,
for his gracious encouragement. Chapter 5 was written for a collection
of essays on the subject of religious fundamentalism. It has appeared
previously in the volume *Fundamentalisms* edited by Christopher
Partridge (Carlisle: Paternoster Press, 2001) and is used here by kind
permission of the publishers. The material in chapter 6 was originally
prepared for a conference held at Swanwick on the subject of mission
in modern Africa and sponsored by a number of mission organizations, including Action Partners, Africa Inland Mission and SIM
International. Finally, chapter 8 consists of material presented to the
International Council of SIM at their triennial meetings at the Blue
Ridge Conference Center in North Carolina in 2003 and I am deeply
grateful to Jim Pluedemann and Malcolm MacGregor for the generous

hospitality given to me at these meetings. The participants in this conference, who were wrestling honestly and creatively with many of the issues raised here, offered stimulating and encouraging feedback on this material and I am profoundly thankful for the privilege of enjoying their fellowship.

In conclusion, I must thank the theological books editor of Inter-Varsity Press, Philip Duce, for his constant advice and encouragement in the production of this volume. The book certainly would not have seen the light of day without Philip's friendship, wisdom and editorial skills and I am deeply grateful to him.

David Smith
International Christian College, Glasgow
April, 2003

1 Global Christianity and the healing of the nations

Almost one hundred years ago a book appeared which dealt with the prospects for the Christian mission in the new century which had then just begun. Looking back at the long reign of Queen Victoria, the author noted that the entire world had been opened up by European explorers, engineers and traders. China, Asia and Africa had all been brought within the sphere of European political and economic power, and the writer concluded that the nations 'which are best fitted to send Missionaries abroad are the strongest and most influential in the world, and their united empires comprise the greater part of the habitable world'.[1]

The author was certainly correct in his estimate of the extent of the spread of Western power across the world. It has been calculated that by this time the European nations and their former colonies in the Americas had established political and economic control over an

---

1. J. I. Macdonald, *The Redeemer's Reign: Foreign Missions and the Second Advent* (London: Marshall & Scott, 1910), pp. 218–219.

astonishing 84% of the land surface of the globe. After the First World War, the dismemberment of the Ottoman Empire and its division between Britain, France and Italy actually increased this percentage. The British alone claimed possession of an empire 'on which the sun never set', extending their control over 11 million square miles and 390 million people.[2]

Underlying this extraordinary expansion was the conviction of the superiority of Western civilization to all other cultures and world-views. Indeed, the terminology used at the time divided the world between 'civilized' and 'uncivilized' regions, implying that the West alone possessed the gift of civilization which was to be shared with other peoples. Many Christians assumed that the scientific and technological advances made in Europe were in some sense the fruit of the gospel, and they thus treated evangelization and civilization as two interrelated aspects of the mission of the church. Thus, an advocate of missions writing in 1910 could argue that 'steam and electricity' had brought the world together and created a situation in which the church 'has well within her control the power, the wealth, and the learning of the world'.[3] Within a few years this boundless confidence would disappear, but at the time it seemed obvious that the West had a responsibility to both civilize and evangelize humankind in a movement that appeared to be an entirely one-way process.

Within the space of a very few years the terrible carnage of the First World War brought about a radical change of mood and perception, a change reflected in the title of Oswald Spengler's multi-volume work, *Decline of the West*. The confidence of many Western thinkers was now seeping away as communist revolutions and the spread of the Marxist critique of capitalism were beginning to split the world into two armed, ideological camps. As the twentieth century

---

2. See Samuel P. Huntington, *The Clash of Civilizations and the Remaking of World Order* (London: Touchstone Books, 1998), p. 51.
3. Macdonald, *The Redeemer's Reign*, p. 231.

unfolded the dominance of the West was challenged and a bipolar structure emerged in global politics in which rival ideologies faced each other from East to West and endeavoured to align the rest of the world behind their particular version of modernity. Remarkably, as we now look back on the twentieth century, that bipolar structure of world politics has also slipped away into history, leaving us to come to terms with a new world in which we struggle to make sense of a confused global picture.

Of course, for those cultural commentators who have interpreted the apparent triumph of Western liberal democracy as marking the 'end of history' there is no uncertainty or confusion. Such commentators hail the globalization of the market economy and the spread of liberal concepts of democratic government in language that sounds rather like a secular form of the gospel. Those who argue in this way see no alternative future for the peoples of the world apart from the penetration of Western market values into every corner of the globe. This kind of talk contains an uncanny echo of the language of our author from 1910, as though, after an unfortunate hiatus resulting from the Soviet and Chinese resistance to 'progress' in the twentieth century, the whole world again lies open to the civilizing influence of the Western powers. There is, however, one very significant contrast between those who speak in this way today and the situation which existed a century ago: in Europe the linkage between the Christian mission and this project has been broken, revealing the essentially secular and materialist nature of the movement toward globalization.

Clash of civilizations?

According to the American political scientist Samuel Huntington the situation we face in the post-cold war era is very different from that described by the people who assume the 'triumph of the West'. It is, Huntington says, 'sheer hubris to think that because Soviet communism has collapsed, the West has won the world for all time and that Muslims, Chinese and others are going to rush to embrace Western liberalism as the only alternative'. The cold war division of humanity is over, but according to Huntington, it is being replaced, not by a homogeneous, monochrome culture with its roots in Europe and America, but rather by the re-emergence of the fundamental ethnic, religious and civilizational divisions of humanity.[4] Samuel Huntington argues, in my view convincingly, that we are living through a phase in human history in which the long period of Western dominance is ending, and is being replaced by a new world in which there are 'intense, sustained, and multidirectional interactions among all civilizations'. Or, to put it another way, 'the expansion of the West' has ended and the 'revolt against the West' has begun.[5]

My purpose in this chapter is to explore this new and confusing world and to ask, in particular, what the prospects for Christianity and its mission are in this context? If at the beginning of the twentieth century, mission was linked to the civilizing task of powerful Western nations, where does it stand today in a fragmenting world in which other religions and ancient civilizations are resurgent and are increasingly mounting resistance to the spread of the secular values of the West?

I want to go back to the finals of the football World Cup in Japan and Korea in June 2002. At one level this event seemed to illustrate the process by which the entire world is being unified around values and symbols originating in the West. Asians, Africans and Latin Americans are, so it appears, football crazy, with megastars like David Beckham achieving the status of international icons. However, look more closely and you discover evidence of the reality of ethnic and cultural differences. The Korean crowds were enthusiastic, yet orderly to the point of regimentation. Apparently the Dutch coach of the South Korean team was astounded to discover that his players refused to display joy in the dressing room after their remarkable victories for fear of offending the substitutes who had failed to make the

---

4. Huntington, *The Clash of Civilizations*, p. 51.

5. Ibid., p. 53.

team. Quite clearly, deeply embedded cultural values were at work here, so that football was being embraced while also being changed within this Asian context.

There is one other memory from the World Cup Finals worth recalling. After their predictable victory, the entire Brazilian squad, many of whom removed their national strips to reveal T-shirts bearing the slogan 'Jesus loves you', linked hands and knelt together in a very public act of thanksgiving and worship. The British TV commentator was nonplussed by this extraordinary sight, mumbling: 'There seems to be some kind of religious ceremony going on here.' Secular media people in the West are not used to seeing God brought into the sphere of professional sport in this way and are likely to interpret such acts as bizarre, or even unacceptable. However, in that moment in Japan, the Brazilians revealed an aspect of the emerging world picture which is invariably overlooked by Western commentators (including, I am bound to say, Samuel Huntington), namely the emergence and significance of non-Western Christianity.

Modernity and secularization

I will return to the subject of world Christianity shortly, but I want first to notice the significance of the growing realization among Western scholars that certain crucial assumptions regarding the culture of modernity may be false and misleading. It has long been assumed that modernization is a process which brings such massive benefits that peoples everywhere in the world will wish to embrace it. What is more, it has seemed inevitable that nations taking the path of modernization will have to pay a price for this in terms of increasing secularization. Since this has clearly been the experience of the West, especially of Europe, it has been assumed that modernity must always result in the replacement of traditional, communal values with the anonymous and impersonal relationships that are part and parcel of a developed, rationalized society. What is more, the advance of science and technology will inevitably mean the retreat of religion and the removal of God from the public sphere of life. Modernity and secularization (it is thought) belong together and you simply cannot have one without the other.

However, such assumptions seem to be challenged, if not actually falsified, by recent history. The Islamic resurgence reveals a religious response to the secular and materialist values of the West in which there is a selective use of modern science and technology. Islam seems to be perfectly capable of producing competent scientists, technicians and doctors who remain passionate in their devotion to Allah and show no signs of capitulating to Western social values. Indeed, the Muslim terrorists who flew passenger aircraft into the Twin Towers in New York were well trained in the technical and scientific aspects of navigation and flying, but this had not in the least eroded their religious convictions, nor had it diminished their hatred of Western, secular values. Consequently, as Huntington says, it seems increasingly clear that modernization can be separated from Westernization and, rather than weakening ancient cultures and civilizations, it is being used to strengthen them. 'In fundamental ways, the world is becoming more modern and less Western.'[6]

The significance of global Christianity

The Islamic resurgence has been the subject of a great deal of research and comment and the impression is sometimes given that a new form of bipolarity is emerging in which the West may end up defining itself against Islam. Clearly, the challenge of Islam is enormous and must be taken seriously, but what is often overlooked is the fact that Christianity has experienced explosive growth in the

6. Ibid., p. 78. On the challenge which non-Western religious vitality poses for the received paradigm of secularization, see Grace Davie, *Europe: The Exceptional Case. Parameters of Faith in the Modern World* (London: Darton, Longman & Todd, 2001).

Southern hemisphere and is likely to play a significant role in the emerging world order. Despite the fact that the gospel often arrived in Africa, Asia and Latin America in a cultural wrapper that was far from attractive, millions of people on those continents have proved able to separate the treasure from its container and the person and message of Jesus Christ have repeatedly demonstrated an appeal quite distinct 'from the imperial power by which it was originally carried'.[7]

The figures are simply mind-blowing: in the early decades of the twenty-first century the Archbishop of Canterbury will preside over a flock of 150 million Anglicans worldwide, of whom the vast majority are in the Southern hemisphere, including 20 million in Nigeria alone. The State Department in Washington has estimated (and probably over-estimated) the number of Christians in China at 100 million, while the Roman Catholic Church claims 424 million baptized adherents in Latin America. The massive surge of Pentecostal religion in Africa and South America has been seen by some commentators as an event similar in scale and significance to the eighteenth-century Great Awakening and as a movement that is reshaping religion in the twenty-first century.[8] We may argue over

7. Philip Jenkins, *The Next Christendom: The Coming of Global Christianity* (New York: Oxford University Press, 2002), p. 58.

8. The positive assessment of Pentecostalism is found in various works of David Martin, including *Pentecostalism: The World Their Parish* (Oxford: Blackwell, 2002), and in Harvey Cox's important work *Fire From Heaven: The Rise of Pentecostal Spirituality and the Reshaping of Religion in the Twenty-First Century* (Reading, Mass.: Addison-Wesley Publishing, 1995). See also Bernice Martin, 'From Pre- to Postmodernity in Latin America: the case of Pentecostalism', in Paul Heelas (ed.), *Religion, Modernity and Postmodernity* (Oxford: Blackwell, 1998), pp. 102–146. On the other hand, Paul Freston's *Evangelicals and Politics in Asia, Africa and Latin America* (Cambridge: Cambridge University Press, 2001) suggests that detailed empirical, regional studies leave open the question of the social impact of the new churches. Steve Brouwer, Paul Gifford and

the meaning of the statistics, but the fact is that the exponential growth of Southern Christianity is increasingly recognized as a phenomenon of world historical significance which will have huge political as well as religious consequences.

I want to consider the implications of this situation for the churches in the Northern hemisphere, but before we do that, we need to take note of another factor of crucial significance in the emerging world picture. When the author quoted at the start of this chapter wrote confidently about the spread of civilization in 1910, the peoples of Europe, Russia and North America accounted for 32% of the world population. In the year 2000, this figure had almost halved, to 18%, and demographers now predict that by the middle of this century the population of the Northern regions will make up as little as 10% of the peoples of the world. In a recent article, Martin Jacques observed that the clearest indication of the erosion of traditional social ties within the West is to be seen in contemporary attitudes toward children and child-bearing. Jacques also noted that the birth-rate in Europe was now below 1.7, 'far short of the level at which a society naturally replenishes itself'.[9] By contrast, exactly the reverse is happening across the Southern hemisphere. By 2050 India and China will be by far the most populous nations on earth and countries like Indonesia, Nigeria, Pakistan, Brazil, Bangladesh, Ethiopia and Congo will have massive populations.

When the growth of Christianity and Islam is placed in this context, we end up with a situation in which a largely secular First World seems likely to find itself confronting rapidly increasing Southern populations among whom religion continues to thrive and

---

Susan Rose reach more clearly negative conclusions as the title of their book suggests: *Exporting the American Gospel: Global Christian Fundamentalism* (New York: Routledge, 1996).

9. Martin Jacques, 'The Age of Selfishness', *The Guardian*, 5 October 2002, p. 24.

expand.[10] What is more, the majority of the churches in the South will be churches of the poor and as the century unfolds they are likely to be increasingly restive about the manifest injustice of a global system that results in an imbalance 'between where the people are and where the wealth is'. Small wonder then that the United States' intelligence community has begun to recognize the potential danger to American strategic interests posed by people it describes as 'activists' within both Islam and Southern Christianity, people who, according to an official website, 'will emerge to contest such issues as genetic manipulation, women's rights, and the income gap between rich and poor'.

Christianity in the Third World: the view from the South

It is obviously dangerous and misleading to generalize about a phenomenon as complex and diverse as Southern Christianity, not least because there are conflicting interpretations of the data available to us. Yet, while recognizing the risks involved here, I want to suggest that there are some features of non-Western churches that can, with reasonable confidence, be identified as characteristic of Southern Christianity overall.

For example, whatever particular ecclesiastical traditions may be involved, Christians in Africa, Asia and Latin America invariably promote the strange idea that God intervenes directly in everyday life. Kefa Sempangi has described how, amid the terror of Idi Amin's brutal reign in Uganda, he came to realize the importance of reading the gospel within the African context. A desperately poor woman came to him with the request that he and his elders might pray that God would provide her with a Vono bed (a brand well known in parts of Africa, identified with a simple metal bedframe and a basic mattress). 'I could hardly believe my ears', he said: 'It seemed

---

10. See Jenkins, *The Next Christendom*, pp. 80ff.

especially strange now, when our whole country was in serious
trouble . . . Surely we had more pressing things to think about!' But
the following Sunday the woman showed up in church dancing with
excitement. Sempangi sent an usher to find out what the commotion
was about, at which the woman shouted out: 'The kingdom of God
has come! The kingdom of God has come! *Jesus has given me a Vono
bed!*' After hearing many testimonies of this kind from poor
Christians, Sempangi concluded:

> These testimonies caused me to read again the story of Jesus' earthly minis-
> try. The more I read and reflected on his life, the more I saw the naked
> inadequacy of my own approach to the gospel. *I* met people at the point of
> my expertise, my knowledge of the Bible. *Christ* met people at the point of
> their need.[11]

The phenomenal growth of indigenous forms of Pentecostalism
throughout the Southern hemisphere, and especially in Latin America,
must be understood in relation to beliefs like these. People facing a
daily struggle to survive will find little to help them in a Christianity
that is carefully confined to the intellectual sphere and sealed off
from the concrete realities of everyday existence. As Philip Jenkins
says, churches in the Southern continents 'can read the Bible in a way
that makes Christianity look like a wholly different religion from
the faith of prosperous advanced societies of Europe or North
America'.[12]

Theology from the South

Perhaps the crucial difference between Christianity in Western

---

11. Kefa Sempangi, *Reign of Terror, Reign of Love* (Tring: Lion Publishing, 1979),
    pp. 76–78.

12. Jenkins, *The Next Christendom*, p. 217.

Europe and the form the faith is now taking in the Southern continents concerns the impact of the movement known as the Enlightenment on the spirituality, worship and theology of the older churches. For the past few centuries the churches of Europe found themselves responding to the impact of new ideas in philosophy and science, with the inevitable result that theology in the West became highly contextual. As they endeavoured to translate Christian beliefs into Enlightenment categories, Western theologians accepted the existence of a clear distinction between the realms of the sacred and the secular, and they granted a privileged place to rational thought and investigation as the path to knowledge. Theology involved the systematic articulation of belief, biblical interpretation and preaching was to be logical, and truth itself came to be understood in terms of propositions requiring mental assent. As we have seen, it was long assumed that this form of Christianity was capable of meeting the spiritual needs of peoples everywhere, so that missions became the means by which a more or less secularized form of faith was transmitted to the rest of the world. What is now clear is that a theology that exalted the cerebral above the instinctual, gave priority to the individual over the communal, and accepted that matters of faith and ethics were private concerns, contributed to the loss of faith in what was once known as 'Christendom', even as it was being rejected as inadequate to the real needs of growing churches in the new heartlands of Christianity.

What all this implies is that the new centres of living and dynamic theology in the twenty-first century will emerge in those new heartlands of the faith in Africa, Latin America and Asia. As Andrew Walls points out, most African Christians operate within a world-view that is vastly different from that which shapes Western culture. He concludes that the real strength of African Christianity is to be found in its independence from the tradition of the Enlightenment, 'its openness to the accommodation of other visions of reality, visions in which the frontier with the spiritual world is crowded with traffic in both directions, visions which involve communal solidarity and do not take the autonomy of the individual as the defining category'.[13]

Peering into the future

Consider then a possible scenario of the world in 2025. I stress that this is uninspired speculation, not prophecy. Nonetheless, in the light of the facts we have considered, it is not an impossible fantasy. If present trends continue, the Northern hemisphere will be populated by people who are incredibly wealthy, yet find it ever more difficult to articulate the meaning of life in any coherent manner. While the material prosperity of these people continues to grow, protected by massive Government spending on increasingly sophisticated weapons, their numbers will be in sharp decline as birth-rates fall. Immigration from South to North will accelerate because, as a Hispanic theologian has pointed out, 'When the rivers of wealth flow in one direction, it is only natural for the population to flow in the same direction.'[14] By this time though, the shrinking and greying of the indigenous populations in Europe and North America will mean that increased immigration will provide the only way to recruit the labour force required to maintain businesses and services in this privileged part of the world. The French Government recently issued a highly sensitive report which argued that in the coming half-century, Europe will have no alternative but to admit 75 million immigrants and face the consequences of becoming an ethnically mixed society in which growing cultural cross-fertilization is bound to occur.

---

13. Andrew F. Walls, 'Of Ivory Towers and Ashrams: Some Reflections on Theological Scholarship in Africa', *Journal of African Christian Thought*, 3/1 (June 2000), p. 1.

14. Justo L. Gonzalez, *For The Healing of the Nations* (New York: Orbis Books, 1999), p. 83.

Across the Atlantic, by mid-century no less than 100 million Americans will be people of Hispanic origin and 60 million will claim Mexican descent. Meantime, in the Southern hemisphere, vast masses of poor people will wave flags not of communist revolution, but of ascendant Islam and Christianity. There will be huge Christian communities in Brazil, Mexico, Nigeria, Korea, the Philippines and China. However, if the two worlds, North and South, continue to drift apart economically, the danger is that a huge gap will open up at the level of perception and understanding. On the one side, as Philip Jenkins observes, it is easy to anticipate that the Western media will depict the faith of Christians in the South as fanatical, superstitious and sexually repressive. A supernaturalist form of religion that insists on bringing God into politics, economics, and even football, will be parodied as 'jungle religion' and the nations of the old Christendom will be in danger of defining themselves against both Islam and Christianity. Meantime, as the Southern churches become more radical, they will be tempted to view the global situation in apocalyptic terms, and may come to view the rich and selfish North as the last terrible manifestation of Babylon.

Hearing the voice of the Spirit

I propose that in a context like this the most urgent challenge confronting the church worldwide, is that Christians in both North and South should listen to each other and, in fellowship together, hear what the Spirit is saying to them. I am here deliberately alluding to a text that occurs at the end of each of the seven letters to the churches in Revelation 2 and 3. The challenge facing those churches seems to be remarkably similar to that which we face in the twenty-first century. It seems clear that, by the close of the New Testament, most of the 'older' churches addressed in these chapters were deeply compromised by their association with the imperial power of the Roman empire. They were extremely rich and, as one of them boasted, 'did not need a thing'. They were located at the heart of an empire which became prosperous at the expense of the rest of the world and maintained its privileged position by means of the most efficient and ruthless military machine the world had ever seen. Many Christians living in Roman cities or ports operated within this system and so were inclined to believe Roman propaganda and to seek a synthesis between Christ and Caesar. The Laodiceans, the false prophetess Jezebel, the Nicolaitans, all have in common the attempt to adapt and modify Christianity in a way that would make possible their continued involvement in Roman social and economic life, evading the sacrifice and suffering that, according to John of Patmos, are the cost of following the Lamb of God.

In this situation, the risen Christ summons people to 'hear what the Spirit says to the churches' (Rev. 2:7, 11, etc.). Notice that the Holy Spirit is alive and contemporary; the call is not to remember what the Spirit has said in the past (important as that undoubtedly is), but to be open to the voice of God now, today. At the same time, Christians are reminded that this process of listening, of discerning the will of God, involves the fullest possible ecumenical fellowship, since they are to receive both the revelation given to them and the content of the letters delivered to the other churches. No one church has a monopoly on the truth and the wider our fellowship in the Gospel the more likely it is that we shall be able to 'discern the mind of Christ'.

The issue of the unity of Christians is absolutely vital in the context we have attempted to describe. In the nineteenth century, the unity that had been promised by the Great Awakening disappeared as the class divisions of industrial society split the church into denominations which merely reflected and sanctified wider social distinctions. This was the view of Richard Niebuhr who, in a classic study entitled *The Social Sources of Denominationalism,* observed that denominations are sociological groups 'whose principle of differentiation is to be sought in their conformity to the order of social classes and castes'. They represent the secularization and moral failure of Christianity and 'unless the ethics of brotherhood can gain the victory over this divisiveness within the body of Christ it is useless to expect it to be victorious in the world'.[15]

The great danger today is that as the world fractures along cultural and civilizational lines, Christians will again find themselves forced into opposing camps, so that instead of resisting wider social and political trends, they mimic these and even claim that Christ supports their particular civilizational inheritance. The greatest danger of all is that the North–South divide will split the Christian movement, turning Christianity in Europe and America into an ideology in support of privilege, power and wealth, while leaving the Southern churches alienated, bitter and perhaps tempted by the appearance of some latter-day Karl Marx.

How does the message of the book of Revelation relate to this situation? In a remarkable study, the Hispanic historian and theologian Justo Gonzalez has argued that John of Patmos faced exactly the kind of issues we have described. John is summoned to speak to churches that are wealthy, privileged and deeply compromised concerning 'many peoples, nations, languages and kings' (Rev. 10:11). This is a God-given vision of an *alternative* community to the one centred on Rome. Joining this multi-ethnic community brings no guarantee of wealth and security, rather it is likely to lead to suffering and death. Those who follow the Lamb will be involved in witness that is joyful, yet profoundly counter-cultural in the context of an empire that declares itself to be the final goal of human history. Yet it is precisely as Christians catch this vision and see through the blasphemous pretensions of the empire, that they are able to bear faithful witness to the Crucified One who alone holds 'the keys of death and of Hades' (Rev. 1:18). This message of a new, multinational community, united in the worship of the slain and risen Christ, had to be preached to the deeply compromised Christians in Asia Minor. This was not an easy task, since the vision of a multi-ethnic church which stood in total

---

15. H. Richard Niebuhr, *The Social Sources of Denominationalism* (New York: Meridian Books, 1929), p. 25.

contrast to the dominant power and values of Rome, would be resisted and resented by Christians who were prospering by operating within the system.

I want to conclude by quoting from Justo Gonzalez, who demonstrates the significance of the message of the book of Revelation in an age of growing cultural conflict. The future of Christianity in the Northern hemisphere will, it seems to me, be determined by the extent to which rich and privileged Christians can truly hear words like these, and recognize in them what the Spirit is saying to the churches today. This is not to say that Christianity in the South is beyond criticism, or that we have nothing to offer to our sisters and brothers there, but I suggest that our spiritual health depends crucially on how far we can respond to Southern voices like this one. Failure at this point may mean the removal of the candlestick by the Head of the Church. Here then, is Justo Gonzalez' challenge:

> The fact is that the gospel *is* making headway among the many tribes, peoples and languages – that it is indeed making more headway among them than it is among the dominant cultures of the North Atlantic. The question is not whether there will be a multicultural church. Rather, the question is whether those who have become accustomed to seeing the gospel expressed only or primarily in terms of those dominant cultures will be able to participate in the life of the multicultural church that is already a reality.[16]

'He who has an ear, let him hear what the Spirit is saying to the churches.'

---

16. Gonzalez, *For The Healing of the Nations*, p. 91.

2 The shape of holiness in the twenty-first century

My purpose in this chapter is to attempt to explore what is implied by the phrase 'practical holiness' in a world like ours, shaped, as it undoubtedly is, by the powerful forces which underlie the movement we have come to know as 'globalization'. I want discuss this question within the historical context of the beginnings of the Keswick movement, observing the tensions surrounding the issues then before considering their implications in the very different world of the twenty-first century.

First though, let me anticipate a possible objection to the view, implicit within the title of this chapter, that holiness may, indeed should, take different forms at different times and in contrasting social and cultural contexts. If Christian holiness is fundamentally a biblical concept, it might be argued, then surely it will be expressed and lived out in ways that are identical at all times. The standards of God's law and the example of the life of Jesus never change, and these remain our models and guides for life in the twenty-first century, just as they were for Christians living in the Roman empire, or in the so-called 'Dark Ages' in medieval Europe, or in a village in some remote part of Asia relatively untouched by modernity today. Would we not be able to recognize sisters and brothers living holy lives wherever and whenever we met them in this world?

These are important questions and they stem from an entirely valid concern to avoid a cultural relativism that can endanger the absolute values and standards revealed to us in the gospel. The pattern of Christian holiness finds its source in the Christ who is Lord over all cultures and who calls people to follow him from every period of human history. Thus, the apostle Paul, who understood as well as anyone the need for the translation of the gospel into the idioms and forms of different cultures, described the ultimate aim of his ministry as to so proclaim Christ as to 'present everyone perfect' in him (Col. 1:28). Thus, at all times and in every culture, Christian holiness involves following Jesus, reproducing something of his purity and compassion, and bearing witness to the disturbing values of the kingdom he came to unveil.

Having said this, holiness is (as the Keswick movement always stressed) a practical affair, related in a vital and real way to the concrete and specific issues that arise for Christians in their particular time and place. It is not something abstract and timeless, but is shaped in its expression and forms by the principle of the incarnation which lies at the very heart of the gospel. Consequently, to 'be holy' – to reflect the likeness of Christ – demands of all Christians that they relate their confession of Jesus as Lord to the actual situation within which they exist. To fail to do this by, for example, retaining the forms of holiness inherited from a previous generation at a time of massive cultural change, is to undermine practical holiness and to evade the real challenge of discipleship.

Let me illustrate what this means in practice. One of the great examples of the contextualization of faith and holiness in a non-Western cultural setting is to be found in the extraordinary life of the Indian Christian mystic, Sadhu Sundar Singh. Devoted to Jesus and determined to take the spiritual and ethical teaching of his Master with utter seriousness, Sundar Singh separated Christ from the

Western forms of theology and discipleship with which he had so often been associated (one might say, imprisoned). The Sadhu incarnated the gospel in a manner that made visible and real the life-giving power of Jesus in the context of the Hindu-shaped culture of India. On a visit to England this Asian holy man arrived at a large country house and rang the doorbell. A young maid answered the door and looked in some astonishment at the dark, saffron-clad stranger who stood before her. Although he announced his name, the young woman fled in some confusion to the lady of the house and declared: 'There's a man at the door: I don't know his name, but he looks like Jesus.'

The story illustrates exactly the balance we need in relation to the essence and forms of Christian holiness: the forms are various, contextual and concrete, while the essence always involves 'looking like Jesus'. The challenge I want to address here is precisely this: what will it mean in practice to reflect Jesus, or as John puts it, 'to walk as Jesus did' (cf. 1 John 2:6), in a world like ours today?

Holiness as a disputed concept

The difficulties of understanding the nature of the relationship between Christianity and culture, and between the expression of Christian holiness and culture, can be illustrated from the emergence of the Keswick movement in the 1870s. There is a good deal of evidence to suggest that those involved in founding the Convention belonged to a troubled and anxious generation. Many testimonies from these years indicate that Christians were experiencing growing tensions between their expectations of the Christian life, on the one hand, and the realities of failure, compromise and unhappiness which seemed to be their normal daily experience, on the other. Those who attended the first conventions confessed that, before their discovery of the 'victorious life', they were beset by problems such as being 'plagued by an ugly temper', or 'giving way to irritation', or acting in unlovely ways toward 'people who are very trying'.

Those who came to Keswick 125 years ago openly confessed that such failures led to their Christian lives being dogged by constant worry and anxiety.

In this context, two books originally published in America were read avidly in the United Kingdom and set in motion a series of meetings and conferences from which the Keswick movement sprang. W. E. Boardman's *A Higher Life* and Mrs Hannah Whitall-Smith's *The Christian's Secret of a Happy Life* described how the authors had discovered a new level of Christian existence. Hannah Whitall-Smith's book in particular struck a chord with middle- and upper-class British evangelicals. She had herself been challenged by someone who had asked her why it was that Christians seemed to be such utterly miserable people! She knew that this claim was not without foundation, but she could also testify to an experience which so transformed the Christian life that it enabled believers to rebut such statements. She and her husband, Robert, preached a gospel of victory; they had discovered the secret that Christ could indeed lift believers onto a higher plane and enable them to escape from the slough of despond.

At the time this approach to Christian holiness seemed to be an innovation and was in fact highly controversial. Bishop J. C. Ryle deplored the 'love of novelty' which he detected in the new move-ment and he lamented the tendency to despise older approaches to holiness derived from the English Puritans. 'There is', Ryle said, 'an incessant craving after any teaching that is sensational, and excit-ing, and rousing to the feelings. There is an unhealthy appetite for a sort of spasmodic and hysterical Christianity.'[1] In a memorable phrase, Ryle protested that the new approach to spirituality intro-duced by people like the Whitall-Smiths was 'little better than spiritual dram-drinking'. An even more serious charge was that the families of people who claimed to have received the 'higher life'

---

1. J. C. Ryle, *Holiness: Its Nature, Hindrances, Difficulties and Roots* (London: James Clarke, 1952), p. xvii.

often saw no evidence of improvement in their behaviour in the home, and as a result 'immense harm is done to the cause of Christ'.

What was the historical and social context within which these controversial changes were taking place? What was it about the situation in Britain in the 1870s that resulted in evangelicals feeling so anxious and unhappy? And how might we explain the widespread feeling of failure which provided the fertile soil within which the preachers of the new message of the 'higher life' could reap such an extraordinary harvest? Despite his criticisms of Keswick, Ryle himself was well aware of the troubled nature of the times and he freely acknowledged that the religious condition of the country seemed to be quite dreadful. Less than a hundred years earlier, evangelicals had been supremely confident that they stood on the edge of a period of unprecedented blessing in which the gospel would transform the entire world, but that kind of optimism had gradually drained away throughout the nineteenth century. The work of C. H. Spurgeon illustrates this well; after preaching an optimistic theology throughout his ministry, he was overwhelmed by pessimism at the end of his life and shared Ryle's sense of gloom concerning the trends he saw in both church and society.

The fact is that in Europe and the United States, evangelicals in the last quarter of the nineteenth century were facing multiple pressures. First, there was the emergence of what was called 'modern thought' which was spreading throughout the Western world and seemed to undermine traditional belief in the veracity and authority of the Bible. The new sciences, especially biology and palaeontology, seemed to challenge the inherited world-view and evangelicals struggled to come to terms with the fact that their most cherished beliefs were being dislodged from the heart of Western culture. As a result, a gap opened up between the generations and many children from evangelical families found themselves facing a severe crisis of faith. In a classic account called *Father and Son*, Edmund Gosse described how he found himself moving almost imperceptibly away from his father's beliefs, and this generational split was experienced in many evangelical homes.[2] The word 'agnosticism' came into the English language at this time to describe a generation reared in devoutly Christian homes, but now alienated from the certainties of their parents and wrestling with profound religious doubts. On the side of the parents, this was obviously a major cause of the anxiety and unhappiness to which attention has been drawn.

Second, the seemingly intractable 'social problems' posed by sprawling urban centres like London, Sheffield and Glasgow, where thousands of people lived in conditions of squalor and destitution, also fed evangelical fears. Among working-class people there were rising demands for political and social reform which threatened the older hierarchical structures of British society to which many evangelicals appeared to be wedded. Within the emergent labour movement there were calls for the disestablishment of the Church of England, attacks on patronage and privilege, and increasingly stridEnt demands for social justice and universal suffrage, all of which seemed to shake the very foundations of the class structure of British society. The remoteness and tranquillity of Keswick, a town promoted as a resort catering for the elite of Lakeland visitors, offered relief from these pressures. Not surprisingly, very few people from the lower classes were to be found in the Convention audiences at this time. Indeed, when a camp of working men did appear at the beginning of the twentieth century, it drew a rather patronizing comment on the fact that these people were 'mainly factory workers, clerks and artisans'.

Third, and perhaps most serious of all, there were the problems of simply living the Christian life in a society which seemed to be moving in a direction that undermined the fundamental ethical values of the gospel. In the floodtide of modernity and with economic values controlling the public sphere, Christians increasingly found themselves living in two worlds – the private world of family

---

2. Edmund Gosse, *Father and Son* (1907, repr. Harmondsworth: Penguin Books, 1986).

and church, in which Christ was confessed as Lord and the Bible constituted (at least in theory) the supreme authority, and the public world of commerce and business in which the values created by consumer capitalism reigned supreme. Christians who had grown up shaped by the Protestant work ethic now found themselves caught in a terrible tension, since to succeed in the public world they had to be willing to act on the basis of values which seemed to run directly counter to the gospel. In this public world caution and sobriety were being replaced by impulse; thrift and simplicity gave way to the drive to acquire things merely because their symbolic value enhanced one's standing in society; and an awareness of the dangers of money now seemed dated and an obstacle to progress in a society which actively encouraged lavish spending. Middle- and upper-class evangelicals thus experienced a dissonance between the older values of the past and the new practices they encountered daily in business and professional spheres. As a result, says Douglas Frank, God's will, as understood from childhood, and the value-system operating in the wider society 'were beginning to sound like two different things'.[3]

In this situation, the message of the 'higher life', of victory over besetting sins like worry, outbursts of bad temper, and impatience was welcomed since it seemed to speak precisely to the felt needs of those to whom it was directed. It is revealing to discover the kind of sins which were most frequently confessed at this time. They included a 'tattling tongue, angry looks, viciousness on the croquet lawn, impatience with servants'. Women testified that the experience of the 'victorious life' gave them new strength on those days when they 'felt poorly', while their husbands were able to overcome worry about the next bank failure. Robert Pearsall-Smith often spoke to the aristocracy in England's great country houses and in the course of

---

3. Douglas W. Franks, *Less Than Conquerors: How Evangelicals Entered the Twentieth Century* (Grand Rapids: Eerdmans, 1986), p. 140. My discussion of the history of the early Keswick movement draws heavily upon Douglas Franks's excellent work.

one address he asked: 'Does the sudden pull of the bell ever give notice in the kitchen that a good temper has been lost by the head of the household?' The message of the 'victorious life' was evidently directed to those who lived upstairs and it offered them a way to overcome anger with their social inferiors, enabling them to rise above the anxiety and worry that could plague their lives if they dwelt too long on the changes that might be under way downstairs. Despite all the pressures experienced in a secularizing society, one might find in Christ a peace, joy and power which simply lifted the soul above such cares. In Douglas Franks's words, the message of Keswick spoke 'to the spiritual agonies of a troubled Christian generation in its passage to modernity, and it offered that generation . . . an opportunity to transcend its agonies through the Spirit's power to indwell the Christian with a life of perfect victory'.[4]

I would not want the observations made here to be understood in such a way as to imply that I wish to ignore or deny the great good that came from the early Keswick movement. There are, as Bishop Ryle recognized at the time, serious theological questions to be asked about the message of the 'victorious life', and it seems clear that for Victorian evangelicalism the meetings at Keswick represented a 'retreat' in a far more profound and significant sense than was intended by the use of that word. As the historian David Bebbington says, the adherents of Keswick were accepting that evangelicalism, 'which had come so near to dominating the national culture at mid-century, was on the way to becoming an introverted sub-culture'.[5] Nonetheless, many who attended these conventions had religious experiences which resulted in lives of sacrificial service for Jesus Christ, often in the far corners of the globe through the agency of new faith missions, or in the inner cities where, like William and Catherine Booth, they did much to restore the credibility of the

---

4. Ibid., p. 115.

5. David Bebbington, *Evangelicalism in Modern Britain: A History From the 1730s to the 1980s* (London: Unwin Hyman, 1989), p. 180.

gospel among its 'uncultured despisers'. If the early Keswick Convention failed to confront the really difficult issues concerning the practice of Christianity in a society becoming secular and thoroughly materialistic, the question we must face is: are we able to claim any greater success in this regard in the context of the so-called 'new world order' at the start of the twenty-first century?

Holiness in the era of globalization

It is relatively easy with the benefit of hindsight, and with the help of serious historical research, to describe the social context of Victorian Britain and to identify the ways in which Christians failed to engage with some of the critical issues which arose at that time. The crucial issues for us concern the understanding of our times and the response we make now as those who confess Christ as Lord.

I want to focus attention on two aspects of the situation in which we find ourselves today. The first concerns the de-Christianization of our culture. Peter Brierley has described the decline of institutional Christianity in England in his book *The Tide Is Running Out* in which he likens the loss of members from all Christian traditions as similar to 'a haemorrhage akin to a burst artery'. Brierley notes that Britain 'is full of people who used to go to church but no longer do'.[6] The same conclusions are reached by the Scottish social historian Callum Brown who, in a book with the title *The Death of Christian Britain,* concludes that 'the cycle of inter-generational renewal of Christian affiliation' has been 'permanently disrupted' with the result that 'a formerly religious people have entirely forsaken organised Christianity in a sudden plunge into a truly secular condition'.[7]

---

6. Peter Brierley, *The Tide is Running Out* (London: Christian Research, 2000), p. 236.

7. Callum Brown, *The Death of Christian Britain: Understanding Secularisation 1800–2000* (London: Routledge, 2001), p. 1.

The second important feature of our times concerns the emergence and seemingly unstoppable progress of the phenomenon of globalization. Since the collapse of communism in Eastern Europe and the end of the cold war, a market culture has spread around the globe drawing the whole world and all its peoples within its control. Not surprisingly, this achievement, which so closely resembles the objectives that Christians have always associated with the missionary movement, is increasingly spoken of in language that is overtly religious. Globalization thus involves not merely a particular type of economic activity, but the promotion of a world-view in which human identity is defined in terms of the consumption of goods and the identification of people with particular brands. The global market is thus much more than a merely economic factor in modern life; it extends a particular culture around the world and promotes the view that the consumption of material goods is of the essence of human identity and purpose.

Anyone who doubts this analysis should take note of the kind of claims that are made for manufactured goods in contemporary advertising. In 1988 the American computer giant IBM produced a TV commercial which showed great throngs of humanity going about their business while a tiny caption asked 'Who is everywhere?' In the background the rock group REM played the anthem 'I am Superman' as IBM proceeded to identify itself with the name of God revealed to Moses as the words 'I AM' were held aloft amid the crowds. In the same mood, an advertisement for cellphones suggested that every owner might now claim the divine attribute of omnipresence as it assured customers: 'You are everywhere!' Renault advertised a new model in the 1990s with the words 'The Power' over the car's engine and 'The Glory' over the interior; not content with this, a recent promotional campaign has a black gospel choir leaving a church and gathering round the latest people-carrier to sing its praises. In the early 1990s a whole series of books promoting new management theories employed traditional religious language which suggested that market capitalism had not only defeated communism, but had indeed become the new religion. A best-selling volume in 1992, which had a huge impact on American business thinking, contained a chapter with the title 'The Market's Will Be Done'. Of even greater concern to us is the fact that among the best-selling books on management theory in America in the 1990s were titles like *God Wants You To Be Rich* and *Jesus, CEO*. As one commentator observes, the logic of the 'new economy' has so penetrated every aspect of postmodern Western culture that material and economistic imperatives have overwhelmed and displaced 'every other way of imagining the world'.

We have seen how those who came to the first Keswick Conventions over a century ago belonged to a troubled generation of Christians who felt deeply the tension between their Christian profession and the pressures of a world increasingly shaped by materialist values. We may criticize their response to this situation, but the question we must face is this: are we even aware today that there is a tension between the demands of Christian discipleship and the values which drive the global economy and more and more dominate our lives?

In attempting to respond to this question, I want to consider a text which has played a significant role in defining Christian holiness in the past. The book of Revelation summons the early Christians:

'Come out of her, my people,
so that you will not share in her sins,
so that you will not receive any of her plagues;
for her sins are piled up to heaven,
and God has remembered her crimes.'
(Rev. 18:4–5)

This is obviously a call for separation, a summons to leave a sphere dominated by sin and doomed under the judgment of a just and holy God. It is an invitation to discover a different drumbeat and to join those who, despised and hated as they will be, march in the opposite direction to the masses who trudge toward destruction. The crucial question is: what is the movement, or institution, we are called to leave? In the context of Revelation 18 the reference is to 'Babylon' and the entire chapter contains a chilling prophecy of her fall and total destruction. But this does not help us very much, because we must still decipher the code in order to discover who or what is represented by the verbal symbol 'Babylon'.

It would be interesting to survey the ways in which this question has been dealt with in the history of exegesis, but I simply want to draw on personal memory in recalling that the separation demanded by this text has often been understood to refer to institutions like the Church of Rome, or even the ecumenical movement. In my youth I listened to sermons in which it was simply taken as self-evident that the passage was to be read as a warning against recognizing other professing Christians as true believers. The text was thus used to justify a separatist and sectarian position in the interests of doctrinal and ecclesiastical purity.

Perhaps the most charitable thing one can say about such exegesis is that it was misguided! To its great credit, the Keswick movement set its face against that kind of sectarianism and from its beginnings promoted a broad-based unity encapsulated in the famous slogan 'All One in Christ Jesus'. Perhaps today, in the context of the 'death of Christian Britain', we may be able to discover a new and deeper unity between all Christians in which together, we listen afresh to this disturbing word of God.

The starting-point for a real understanding of this passage must be, I suggest, the question: what did it mean then? The book of Revelation, so puzzling to later readers, is highly contextual and relates very closely to the actual world in which the first readers lived. That world, like ours, was dominated by a global political and economic system whose beneficiaries lauded its achievements in explicitly religious language. I refer of course to the Roman empire which was praised as the ultimate goal of human history – *Roma Aeterna*. The perspective of the book of Revelation is radically different. John's vision is shaped, on the one hand, by his knowledge of the glory of God as revealed in Christ, and, on the other hand, by an awareness of those deeply negative aspects of Roman rule involving the suffering and anguish of people who were the victims of Roman power. These were people whose stories were carefully edited out of the official propaganda. As Richard Bauckham puts it: 'either one shares Rome's own ideology, the view of the Empire promoted by Roman propaganda, or one sees it from the perspective of heaven, which unmasks the pretensions of Rome'.[8] In his brilliant study of the theology of the book, Bauckham shows how it repeatedly subverts Rome's self-understanding, getting beneath the surface to uncover its foundations in acts of violent oppression and economic exploitation. Revelation 18 illustrates this perfectly: it describes the global reach of Rome's economic power, listing the luxurious items sucked into the centre from around the known world, but then suddenly reveals that the glory and prosperity of Rome was achieved at the tremendous cost of 'the bodies and souls of men' (18:11–13).

This is the 'Babylon' from which the followers of the Lamb are called out. Ancient Babylon stands here as a symbol for every system of domination which defies the authority of the holy creator-God and arrogantly announces the end of history in the interests of those who have their hands on the levers of economic and political power. John's first readers had no difficulty in recognizing the Roman empire as a new and powerful manifestation of the evil and idolatrous spirit of 'Babylon'. It was, Bauckham says, 'the Christian vision of the incomparable God, exalted above all worldly power, which relativized Roman power and exposed Rome's pretensions to divinity as a dangerous delusion'.[9]

The inevitable question which arises here is how, in terms of practical holiness, this might apply to us today? Just as in the first century Christians found themselves asking how it could be possible to truly follow Jesus in a world in which the pagan Roman empire filled the horizon, so today we must ask, in all seriousness, whether it is possible to be Christian in the new age of globalization. We may criticize the early Keswick movement for failing to grasp the real agenda posed by the modern world, but are we any more able to be faithful

---

8. Richard Bauckham, *The Theology of the Book of Revelation* (Cambridge: Cambridge University Press, 1993), p. 8.

9. Ibid., p. 39.

in addressing the same, unfinished agenda today? Are Christians in London, Moscow, New York, or Beijing capable of hearing a different drumbeat, of catching an alternative vision to the one which increasingly dominates the entire world?

Practical holiness in the twenty-first century

If the context of the book of Revelation in the Roman empire suggests close parallels with our globalized world today, it is worth noticing that the condition of the churches addressed in this book also sounds rather familiar. We are used to the picture of the earliest churches painted in the book of Acts and are inclined to treat this as the normative pattern of the church in the New Testament. Here we witness congregations experiencing remarkable growth in a blaze of Pentecostal glory, thousands turn to Christ, and in a spontaneous missionary expansion the church crosses the cultural divide between Jew and Greek. This triumphant progress ends with Paul in Rome, where, despite his confinement, we find him teaching the message of the kingdom of God 'without hindrance' (Acts 28:31). With the seed of the gospel successfully planted at the centre of the known world one has the impression that it cannot be long before the task is completed and the end of the age arrives.

But it was not to be so! By the end of the New Testament the picture has changed: the revival fires have died down, the love of many has grown cold, and leaders like John find themselves imprisoned for preaching a subversive message. Surveying this scene a contemporary sociologist might well have written a book with the title, *The Death of Christianity in Asia Minor*. The description of the churches in Revelation 2–3 is a gloomy one and it suggests that they, like us, had found the power of an economistic culture too hard to resist. Here are whole congregations idolizing material prosperity in a manner that exactly mirrored the spirit of Rome. The 'letters to the seven churches' make it clear that leaders and teachers within these congregations were actually urging Christians to accept a synthesis between the gospel and the culture of Rome. The group identified as the Nicolaitans (2:15), for example, were advocating a syncretism which would enable believers to retain the Christian name while ensuring their continued social and economic success within Roman society. Here was a policy similar to that we have noted earlier in this chapter, of limiting Christ's lordship to the private sphere, so that he could be praised within the church while being excluded from the real world in which Caesar called all the shots. The startling truth is, however, that such an accommodation to the Roman world-view results in the living Christ withdrawing his presence even from the church, knocking for admission from the outside (3:20), in a final invitation to individuals who might still be able to recognize his drumbeat.

This is the context within which the call is issued: 'Come out of her, my people' (Rev. 18:4). Earlier in this chapter I quoted a commentator who said that in contemporary Western culture, the imperatives of the market economy have replaced 'every other way of imagining the world'. This was precisely the situation in which John's readers found themselves: the symbols of Roman power dominated the ancient world so completely that the citizens of the empire had internalized the ideology of Rome and simply could not imagine another kind of world. Even today, standing in the ruins of the Colosseum, or entering the extraordinary building known as the Pantheon in Rome, or walking along Hadrian's Wall, one is able to grasp the extent of the achievement of ancient Rome. But, precisely in such a context, the book of Revelation invites Christians to imagine another, quite different world. John's visions expand his readers' world and open it up to a transcendent view of reality. In Bauckham's words, 'The bounds which Roman power and ideology set to the readers' world are broken open and that world is seen as open to the greater purpose of its transcendent Creator and Lord.'[10]

What all this means is that as, 2,000 years after Revelation was written, we follow John through the door that stands open in heaven

10. Ibid., p. 7.

(4:1), we can discover an exit from the insanity of the world in which we live our lives. There is a way out of the madness of our world, an alternative view of humankind and its place in the cosmos. There is a radically different way of understanding ourselves, one that delivers us from the materialism and sheer nihilism which currently leads the world astray. However, that open door provides not only an exit, but also an entrance into another realm where everything is different. On the other side of the door the first thing that comes into view is the throne of God and it is in the light of that vision that the arrogance and folly of 'Babylon' is seen for what it really is. Here it becomes clear that both truth and the ultimate triumph belong to the once-slain Lamb of God. The visions of Revelation are thus life-giving and life-transforming; they lead us from lies and delusions to truth and reality, and they point toward an ultimate goal in which the holy and loving Creator promises to make everything new and finally to eliminate all the causes of human misery and grief. But to catch this vision is to be exposed to great danger, because the church that marches to this very different drumbeat in the context of Babylon becomes a counter-cultural, subversive and even revolutionary force.

The cost of discipleship

We have considered the controversies around the concept of 'holiness' in the 1870s and I have indicated some sympathy for the criticisms that Bishop Ryle made of the early Keswick movement. But there is a sense in which those who advocated the 'higher life' had discovered something important. The visions of Revelation do point to another dimension of reality, above the noise and strife of a world hopelessly addicted to the idols of mammon and eros. But, contrary to the sermons I heard nearly half-a-century ago, the Apocalypse does not advocate sectarian withdrawal into a privatized sphere labelled 'religion'. Rather, it summons the worshipping people of God to follow the Lamb in full view of the watching world, offering a public model of an alternative community which will attract those who are wearied by the lies and deception of Babylon. Crucial to all of this is the worshipping life of the church which, in Richard Bauckham's words, is 'the source of resistance to the idolatries of the public world'.[11] In its purging and renewal of the Christian imagination, and in its sustaining of genuine hope through the anticipation of the time when the true God will be recognized by all the nations, in the worship 'for which the whole of creation is destined', the book of Revelation does indeed sound a 'different drumbeat'. However, marching to that drumbeat involves abandoning the modern Babylon and being ready to face the suffering that is likely to be the lot of counter-cultural subversives. This is why we do not read far into this book before we encounter the martyrs who overcame evil 'by the blood of the Lamb and by the word of their testimony' and who did 'not love their lives so much as to shrink from death' (Rev. 12:11). If the parallels I have suggested here are valid, then Christians in the Western world may need to take the theme of suffering for the sake of Christ far more seriously than they have needed to do for the past 1,700 years.

_____

11. Ibid., p. 161.

3 The theology of revival in global perspective

The subject of the work of the Holy Spirit in revival and the assumption that the primary means of the renewal of the church is through movements of revival, is so central within the evangelical tradition that it might be said to belong to the self-definition of the movement. This is not surprising given the fact that evangelicalism came to birth in the Great Awakening of the eighteenth century. A movement emerging from such a revival naturally made the need for, and the expectation of, times of spiritual revival central to its understanding of the church and its mission in the world. Indeed, evangelicalism has sometimes been described as 'revival Christianity'.

It is important to notice that the prominence given to the role of revivals in the growth of the Christian movement was related to a particular form of eschatological belief which was widely, if not universally, held within the first generation of the evangelical movement. In the second half of the eighteenth century, Christians on both sides of the Atlantic anticipated an age of unprecedented blessing and the hope was strong that the revival experienced in Britain and America would spread around the world and usher in the millennial glory through which peoples everywhere would come to worship and honour the living God. 'A time shall come', wrote Jonathan Edwards, 'when religion and true Christianity shall in every respect be uppermost in the world.' The nations would finally abandon warfare as the ancient prophetic promises of universal love and peace at last became reality and 'the whole earth' would become 'one holy city, one heavenly family, men of all nations [dwelling] together'.[1]

Postmillennial optimism of this kind played a crucial role in the spread of evangelicalism in Britain and America and in the emergence of the modern missionary movement. William Carey reveals the influence of Edwards's extraordinary eschatological vision on the opening pages of his famous *Enquiry* of 1792, arguing that God had 'repeatedly made known his intention to prevail finally over all the power of the Devil' and to extend his own kingdom 'as universally as Satan had extended his'.[2] In other words, Carey takes it for granted that the prophetic Scriptures anticipate an era within human history when Christ will reign over the whole earth and all its peoples. Not only that, the signs of the times seemed to indicate that the world stood on the brink of the dayspring of this golden age when still unfulfilled Old Testament prophecies would at last become reality. An expectation as great as this obviously required powerful movements of revival throughout the world, so that the spiritual awakening that had occurred in Europe and America served as a model for the church, both in its missionary expansion overseas and in its subsequent historical development in the Western world.

---

1. Jonathan Edwards, *The Works of Jonathan Edwards*, vol. 2 (London: Westley and A. H. Davis, 1834), pp. 297–298.
2. William Carey, *An Enquiry into the Obligations of Christians to use Means For the Conversion of the Heathens* (1792, repr. Didcot: Baptist Missionary Society, 1961), p. 5.

The concept of revival in Christian history

It is perhaps surprising to discover that the term 'revival' as it is being used here does not seem to have appeared before the eighteenth century. Iain Murray suggests that it was first used in this sense in the work of Cotton Mather, in which case this particular understanding of 'revivals' would seem to be a modern development.[3] It is possible, nonetheless, to recognize the newness of this terminology while maintaining that the evangelical stress on the renewing activity of the Holy Spirit through revivals was a recovery of an aspect of biblical theology which seems to have escaped the notice of the Protestant Reformers. This is entirely plausible since, as Carey pointed out, those same Reformers had failed to recognize the clear apostolic injunctions to engage in worldwide mission. Geoffrey Best has said that the Evangelical Awakening 'brought the third person of the Trinity back into common circulation'[4] and we may argue that this renewed awareness of the work of the Holy Spirit led to the rediscovery of the biblical phenomenon of revival which had long been neglected within Christendom.

Long neglected – but not previously unknown. Six centuries before Jonathan Edwards developed his remarkable theology of revival and linked this with the hope of an age of universal peace and well-being, Joachim of Fiore (c. 1135–1202) had expounded a Christian vision of history in which a new age of the Holy Spirit would result in love, joy and freedom as 'the knowledge of God would be revealed directly in the hearts of all men'.[5] Joachim did not use the term

---

3. Iain Murray, *Pentecost Today? The Biblical Basis for Understanding Revival* (Edinburgh: Banner of Truth, 1998), p. 3.
4. Geoffrey Best, 'Evangelicalism and the Victorians', in Anthony Symondson (ed.), *The Victorian Crisis of Faith* (London: SPCK, 1970), p. 39.
5. Norman Cohn, *The Pursuit of the Millennium* (London: Paladin Books, 1970), pp. 108–109. See also Anthony Cross, 'The Bible, the Trinity and History: Apocalypticism and Millennialism in the Theology of Joachim of Fiore', in

'revival' to describe the means by which this vision would become historical reality, but his conviction that the outpouring of the Holy Spirit would turn the whole world into a vast monastery in which humankind would be united in the praises of God 'entered into the common stock of European social mythology' and bears a remarkable likeness to the eighteenth-century vision of the early evangelicals.

Thus, if the term 'revival' is new, the phenomenon to which it points is not. Indeed, it could be argued that the Great Awakening, which challenged the highly cerebral form of Christianity known as Deism in the eighteenth century, was the latest eruption of a long tradition of renewal movements by means of which the church has been periodically reminded of its true origin and nature. Such movements always stress the empowering work of the Holy Spirit and the crucial significance of eschatology, both themes likely to be neglected or suppressed by churches primarily concerned with the maintenance of ecclesiastical structure and order, or tempted by an unbalanced intellectualism which defines faith in purely rational categories. Movements like this are, by definition, not gentle and even, but rather erupt into history, revitalizing the church and frequently resulting in significant social and moral transformation. The question that must be asked (and it is one to which I will return) is this: is the current surge of Christianity in the Southern hemisphere, often in a Pentecostal form, simply the latest manifestation of this same tradition?

I want at this point to note the distinction between 'revival' and 'revivalism'. The transition from a belief in revival as an outpouring of the Holy Spirit and, therefore, primarily an act of God, to the nineteenth-century emphasis on revivals as events that could be triggered by appropriate human actions, has often been noted. However, my concern is to observe that even in the context of a Reformed theology stressing divine sovereignty and grace, the danger exists that the category 'revival' can become so dominant in

Stanley Porter et al. (eds.), *Faith in the Millennium* (Sheffield: Sheffield Academic Press, 2001), pp. 260–297.

shaping the understanding of the church and its mission in the world, that it eclipses other important biblical perspectives. In other words, revivalism is not restricted to the Arminian tradition but may also emerge within the framework of a Reformed theology.

Let me try to illustrate what I mean by this in relation to the historical experience of William Carey and his colleagues in India. The correspondence of these pioneers of Protestant mission in the Hindu-shaped culture of India reveals a growing realization that their earlier anticipations of revival in that context were misplaced. Writing to John Ryland in 1800, Carey said: 'I have often thought that it is very probable that we may be only as pioneers to prepare the way for more successful missionaries.'[6] Twenty years later, Carey's co-worker William Ward wrote that 'the restricted progress of Christianity' formed 'one of the most mysterious dispensations of Providence that has ever occupied human attention'.[7] Like almost all the first generation of Baptists in Asia, Ward had gone to India anticipating the imminent spread of millennial glory over the subcontinent but, confronted with the reality of a deeply resistant culture, he was compelled to search for a new model of the church and its mission which would enable him to account for the absence of revival and the strange lack of converts. That quest, I want to suggest, has become common to all of us in the Western world as we seek for a broader understanding which places both revival and decline within the overarching purposes of God.

Biblical foundations for the doctrine of revival

The evangelical belief in the phenomenon of revivals has generally been grounded on appeals to two types of biblical texts. First, and perhaps surprisingly, the doctrine rests upon Old Testament texts in

---

6. William Carey, *The Periodical Accounts*, vol. 2 (1800), p. 75.

7. William Ward, *Farewell Letters* (London, 1821), p. 34.

the Psalms and the Prophets in which the healing, restorative activity of God is promised. For example, in a study of the subject with the subtitle *What the Bible Teaches the Church for Today*, Raymond Ortlund acknowledges that the term 'revival' cannot be found in Scripture in the sense that he wishes to use it, but then claims that the Old Testament clearly contains the idea signified by that word. 'The Scripture is clear, God is able to rend the heavens and come down with unexpected demonstrations of saving power (Isaiah 64).'[8] Like many other writers on this subject, Ortlund assumes rather than demonstrates the connection between the prophetic text he cites and the modern understanding of 'revival'. The deep longing for a greater sense of the presence and power of God among his people, evident on every page of Ortlund's book, is something with which I want to identify without reserve, but I am left asking whether it is self-evident that Isaiah had in view the phenomenon we have come to classify as 'revival'.

The second type of text to which appeal is made relates to the event of Pentecost and the post-Pentecostal works of the Holy Spirit as described in the book of the Acts of the Apostles. Toward the end of his life John Wesley drew a direct comparison between the Great Awakening and the events of Pentecost, arguing that both constituted empirical evidence for the existence and power of God that all reasonable people should acknowledge. In similar vein, the Reformed theologian George Smeaton saw Pentecost as a warrant to pray for further manifestations of divine power, dismissing as 'mischievous and dishonouring to the Holy Spirit' the idea that the day of Pentecost had somehow exhausted the supply of divine life to the church.

Throughout the history of the Christian movement the entrance of new peoples into the kingdom of Christ as the result of the missionary translation of the gospel has been accompanied by experiences of the Holy Spirit so similar to those found in the book of Acts that they have been called 'local Pentecosts'. I recall in this

---

8. Raymond Ortlund Jr, *Revival Sent From God* (Leicester: IVP, 2000), p. 8.

connection my own missionary service in Nigeria, where a powerful spiritual movement among the Annang people in the 1930s
became known locally as the 'Annang Pentecost'. This phrase points
to the recognition of the role played by this crucially important
movement in convincing traditional Africans that the gospel was not
mere 'white man's religion' but was the power of God for salvation
in the specific context of a sub-Saharan primal society. [9] Similar phenomena have been recorded in all parts of the world, often
attracting the attention of anthropologists who have recognized the
social and cultural significance of such 'revitalization' movements.
Thus, the narrative of Pentecost is clearly of fundamental importance to this discussion since it has been understood to contain the
clear promise that the spiritual resources required for the life and
mission of the church in the world will never be withheld from the
people of God.

Central though the story of Pentecost unquestionably is for our
understanding of the nature and calling of the church, it is important to remember that the picture provided by the book of Acts
forms part of a larger narrative of the history of the apostolic
church, not the whole of it. Indeed, as we have noted earlier in this
book, by the close of the New Testament we are looking at a very
different picture: the revival fires have cooled, the love of many has
grown cold, and Christians seem to be increasingly at home in a
world dominated by Roman idolatry and materialism. Certainly, the
Holy Spirit is not absent from this picture, but he comes now not
with the sound of a rushing mighty wind, but with a searching, critical voice, seeking for those, evidently a minority, who are still able
to hear 'what the Spirit is saying to the churches'. Texts like these
must be read alongside the Pentecostal story because, taken
together, they furnish us with the material for a theology of the

---

9. For a detailed description and analysis of this revival, see David Smith, 'A
Survey of New Religious Movements Among the Annang of Nigeria', *Neue
Zeitschrift für Missionswissenschaft* 42.4 (1986), pp. 264–275.

Holy Spirit which enables us to account for decline as well as advance, placing periods of recession and struggle firmly within the divine purpose. This perspective seems especially important for Christianity in the Western world at the present time since our churches look far more like those described in Revelation chapters 2 and 3 than the exploding missionary communities to be found in the book of Acts.

Revival and mission in a globalized world

The topic of revival continues to attract immense interest and concern among contemporary Christians. Despite the gloomy analyses of the state of Western Christianity offered by sociologists and statisticians, a veritable flood of books provide a perspective that can be described as one of 'revivalist optimism'. Rob Warner, for example, articulates a hope which closely parallels the eighteenth-century expectations of the coming of an age of unprecedented, global revival:

> For all the failings and weaknesses of the modern church, we stand at the
> climax of centuries which have seen, step by step, the restoration of the pri-
> orities and practices of the apostolic era. The Spirit of God has surely been
> bringing a continuing reformation to the church in order to equip us for an
> advance unparalleled since the first Christian generation. What is more, the
> globalisation of modern culture and the speed of modern travel together
> provide the opportunity for revival not merely on a national, but on a global
> scale.[10]

Within the Charismatic movement in the West the belief that we now stand on the brink of a movement of global revival that will transcend anything previously experienced is widespread. The

---

10. Rob Warner, *Prepare for Revival* (London: Hodder & Stoughton, 1995), p. 171.

evidence marshalled in support of this positive prognosis includes the phenomenon of the renewal movement itself which, it is claimed, provides an example of 'continuous revival'. The 'Toronto Blessing', although having quickly faded from prominence, is frequently cited as a model of the kind of spiritual stirring which may commence almost anywhere in the world and, through postmodern networks of global communication, can spread rapidly around the planet. In the age of globalization, local awakenings which would once have gone completely unnoticed elsewhere can quickly trigger similar movements on the other side of the globe. Thus, the next 'blessing' may be experienced in Cape Town, Mexico City or Singapore and will then rapidly criss-cross the planet with the potential to encompass the entire human race.

The language used by 'revivalist optimists' is uniformly positive and hopeful. Gerald Coates, for example, takes it for granted that 'we are in the middle of a colossal revival', while R. T. Kendall believes that we stand at the edge of a work of God 'greater than anything heretofore seen' which will lead into 'a post-charismatic era of unprecedented glory'.[11] Rob Warner goes even further, linking 'the greatest revival in the history of the church' with the eschatological hope of the end of the world, arguing that the coming awakening can be identified as that which 'precedes the return of Christ'.[12]

Questions for 'revivalist optimists'

The particular form of revivalism just described prompts a series of questions, the first of which is: is this notion of revival in danger of functioning as a form of religious ideology, concealing the reality of

---

11. Both cited in an unpublished manuscript by Tony Gray, 'An Anatomy of Revival'.

12. Warner, *Prepare for Revival*, p. 171.

the condition of Western Christianity, while also preventing believers from facing the challenges of discipleship and mission in a post-Christian culture? At the end of the 1960s the Dutch theologian J. C. Hoekendijk suggested that calls to evangelism often concealed a lingering nostalgia for the great ages of faith and were motivated by the desire to preserve the crumbling structures of Western Christianity. The evangelistic activities of churches in Europe and North America, he argued, too often concealed the illicit compromises they had made with their host cultures and it was simply nonsense to summon such churches to evangelism 'if we do not call them simultaneously to a radical revision of their life and a revolutionary change of their structure'. To put it bluntly, Hoekendijk said,

> The call to evangelism is often little else than a call to restore 'Christendom'
> . . . as a solid, well-integrated cultural complex, directed and dominated by
> the church. And the sense of urgency is often nothing but a nervous feeling
> of insecurity; with the established church endangered; a flurried activity to
> save the remnants of a time now irrevocably past.[13]

What happens if we apply this analysis to revivalist optimism? Does the focus on revival sometimes conceal a desire to preserve inherited forms of the church and traditional Western theological assumptions, so avoiding the true challenges in *mission* in a radically changed historical and cultural context? The confident announcement that revival is breaking out all around us is reassuring for Christians who are deeply troubled by the loss of a 'Christian culture' and it enables them to hang a 'Business as Usual' sign on the door of the church. If revival is taking place, and if we are assured that it will be the greatest such event experienced in 2,000 years of Christian history, then the radical changes in thought and practice that might be required to engage in the missionary task in a changing culture can be indefinitely postponed.

---

13. J. C. Hoekendijk, *The Church Inside Out* (London: SCM Press, 1967), p. 27.

The connection between revivalism and a Christendom model of the church raises some difficult issues. As we have seen, William Carey discovered that inherited presuppositions concerning revival and evangelism had to be questioned in the light of experience in a non-Christian cultural situation. Consequently, in those parts of the world where Christ had never been named, the category of 'revival' gave way to a new emphasis on 'mission'. The missionary societies that came into being in the nineteenth century were designed to facilitate the spread of the Christian gospel beyond Christendom, with the result that the terms 'revival' and 'mission' came to signify models of the church and its witness appropriate in different geographical locations, one at home, the other overseas.

Throughout the nineteenth century this dichotomy persisted, indeed it hardened. Mission became the form of witness required among primitive peoples who clearly lacked the benefits of a Christian civilization, while evangelism and revival were the means employed to make nominal Western Christians into real believers. Dissenting voices were raised against this distinction and the assumptions on which it rested. Most notably, Søren Kierkegaard launched a blistering attack on Danish Protestant culture-religion, insisting that what went on in the state churches of Europe was a travesty of the gospel of Jesus Christ. In Britain at exactly the same time, Edward Miall had the temerity to suggest that, at the floodtide of their influence, the Victorian churches had actually lost contact with the teaching of Christ and had capitulated to a man-centred religion devoid of spiritual power.[14] At the time these dissenting voices were ignored, but they anticipated by more than a century the perception,

---

14. On Edward Miall, see my 'Church and Society in Britain: A Mid-Nineteenth Century Analysis by Edward Miall', *The Evangelical Quarterly* 61.2 (1989), pp. 141–158. Miall is one of the forgotten prophets of nineteenth-century evangelicalism despite the fact that his 1849 book, *The British Churches in Relation to the British People*, anticipated many of the missionary challenges we now confront.

now common-place, that the demise of the sacral society denoted by the phrase *Corpus Christianum* requires radical rethinking concerning the nature and witness of the churches in the Western world. It requires, in other words, the rejection of the classic distinction between evangelism and revival, on the one hand, and mission on the other. Whatever the prospects for revival may be, the greatest priority of the churches of the West is surely missiological in nature, and this requires a process of biblical reformation through which those churches may become communities 'worthy of attention and respect' and marked by a way of life 'that prompts curiosity, questioning and a new searching'.[15]

The second question prompted by revivalist optimism is: what are the underlying assumptions about the growth, expansion and success of the Christian movement? As we have seen, the first generation of evangelicals was inspired by Jonathan Edwards's vision of an age of blessing that would lead to the evangelization of all peoples on earth. This wonderful prospect found clear expression in the hymns of Isaac Watts and Charles Wesley and was a vital source of Protestant missionary motivation. When Kenneth Scott Latourette began writing his massive seven-volume history of Christian missions in 1937 (a task he completed in 1945), he gave it the title *A History of the Expansion of Christianity*. Clearly, such an idea of Christian missionary progress is compatible with the biblical concern to see the reign of God established throughout the world. Indeed, the tap root of such a concern can be traced to Jesus' instruction to his followers to pray that the will of God might be done 'on earth as it is in heaven'.

However, problems arise when this biblical vision becomes distorted through a one-sided focus on progress and conquest which ignores the reality of setbacks, sufferings and periods of decline and loss which seem to form an integral part of the wider divine purpose in the world.

---

15. Rodney Clapp, *A Peculiar People: The Church as Culture in a Post-Christian Society* (Downers Grove: IVP, 1996), p. 171.

More seriously still, there is a real danger that an optimism that owes more to the secular notion of 'progress' than is often recognized fails to reckon with the terrible reality of the divine holiness in relation to the compromise of the church, and so overlooks the apostolic insistence that judgment begins 'with the family of God' (1 Pet. 4:17).

The great temptation of optimistic revivalism is that it limits the possibility of decline, loss and recession to mere temporary blips in the otherwise inevitable progress toward final and undoubted triumph. The mood of this kind of religion is almost always one of celebration, rarely of lament, with the result that entire swathes of the biblical tradition, in which the faithful pour out their hearts on account of the apparent absence of God and the ambiguities of history, become functionally redundant. Moreover, these scriptural resources are bypassed at a time when precisely such modes of prayer and devotion are most desperately needed by a church which struggles to retain its hold on life 'close to the precipice of death'. This phrase comes from Dietrich Bonhoeffer who, preaching in 1933, on the very day that the German Christians who sought accommodation with Hitler appeared to triumph, provided a biblical and theological perspective on these questions which cannot be bettered:

> We must confess – he [Christ] builds. We must proclaim – he builds. We
> must pray to him – he builds. We do not know his plan. We cannot see
> whether he is building or pulling down. It may be that the times which by
> human standards are times of collapse are for him the great times of build-
> ing. It may be that the times which from the human point of view are
> great times for the church are times when it is pulled down. It is a great
> comfort that Christ gives to his church: you confess, preach, bear witness to
> me, and I alone will build where it pleases me. Do not meddle in what is
> my province.[16]

---

16. Dietrich Bonhoeffer, *No Rusty Swords: Letters, Lectures and Notes, 1928–1936,
   from the Collected Works* (London: Collins/Fontana, 1970), p. 212.

There is a third question which optimistic revivalists should consider very carefully: what are the biblical criteria by means of which we might assess whether or not a movement of revival contributes toward the extension of the reign of God in Jesus Christ? The assumption is sometimes made that any movement identified by the category 'revival' is bound to be a positive phenomenon. Against this, Richard Lovelace warns us that 'the purity of a revival is intimately related to its theological substance. A deep work cannot be done without the sharp instruments of truth.'[17]

Anyone who doubts the correctness of this statement should reflect carefully on the unspeakable tragedy of Rwanda. Christians in all denominational traditions have found themselves asking how it could be that a region of Africa noted for its evangelization and often lauded as an example of 'continuous revival' provided the cultural and ethnic context for a holocaust of unimaginable barbarity and wickedness. A distressed Catholic bishop observed: 'The Christian message is not being heard. After a century of evangelisation we have to begin again because the best catechists . . . were the first to go out with machetes in their hands'.[18] For evangelicals the questions become especially painful, but they lead one missionary to conclude that the massive numerical growth resulting from the East African Revival failed to instil in converts 'a quality of costly discipleship' and resulted in a church that proved 'empty and powerless to confront the pressures of evil'.[19] Roger Bowen says of the tragedy that befell the churches of Rwanda that the issues raised by this experience 'touch us all and nearly all of them impinge all too closely on the churches in the United Kingdom'.[20]

---

17. Richard Lovelace, *The Dynamics of Spiritual Life: An Evangelical Theology of Renewal* (Downers Grove: IVP, 1979), p. 262.

18. Roger Bowen, 'Rwanda – Missionary Reflections on a Catastrophe', *Anvil* 13.1 (1996), p. 36.

19. Ibid., p. 39.

20. Ibid., p. 44.

Dangers confronting 'sociological pessimists'

I turn now to consider an approach to the subject of revival located at the opposite end of the spectrum to that considered above, one which I propose to identify as 'sociological pessimism'. This perspective can be represented by the French Christian thinker Jacques Ellul, who viewed Western Christianity as nothing less than a massive perversion of the gospel of Jesus Christ and argued that, given such apostasy, the present situation could only be understood in terms of the withdrawn-ness and judgment of God. For centuries, Ellul argued, Christianity has been subverted and compromised by its alliance with the culture of Europe, with the result that it became 'the structural ideology of this particular society', abandoning its true calling as 'an explosive ferment calling everything into question in the name of the truth that is in Jesus Christ'.[21]

In a similar vein, Michael Riddell regards talk of revival as an almost insane whistling in the dark. Referring to his native New Zealand, he comments:

> I have lost count of the number of revivalist movements which have swept
> through my homeland promising a massive influx to the church in their
> wake. A year after they have faded, the plight of the Christian community
> seems largely unchanged, apart from a few more who have grown cynical
> through the abuse of their goodwill, energy and money. [22]

Sociological pessimists like Riddell do not dissent from the revivalist assumption that God is still at work in his world, and in the church, but what the revivalists miss is precisely the fact that the divine purpose includes judgment as well as blessing. Indeed, throughout

---

21. Jacques Ellul, *The Subversion of Christianity* (Grand Rapids: Eerdmans, 1986), p. 39.

22. Michael Riddell, *Threshold of the Future: Reforming the Church in the Post-Christian West* (London: SPCK, 1998), p. 14.

Christian history the will of God has often been hidden from human perception and has included times of extreme crisis and decline. Kenneth Scott Latourette, whose magisterial history of Christian missions was noted earlier, understood very well that Christian expansion cannot be marked up on a map of the world in the manner in which multinational businesses chart their progress across the globe. Latourette realized that 'advance and recession, not irreversible progress, was the pattern of Christian expansion, just as Bunyan saw that there was a way to hell even from the gate of heaven'.[23]

For the sociological pessimists then, the category of 'revival' may actually be unhelpful if it is used to pander to the fear and conservatism of those who refuse to move forward into God's new future. In language that echoes that of the revivalists he opposes, Michael Riddell says that 'the Western church stands at the fringes of radically new terrain'. However, what lies beyond this new horizon is not, as the revivalists so often assume, a boom in old-time religion, but the much more difficult and demanding task of a radical reformation which will result in the emergence of quite new models of the church and its mission.

However, just as there are questions to put to the 'revivalist optimists', so too there are real dangers in the position just outlined. The awareness that past glories have gone, that there is an urgent need to adjust our focus and develop new forms of witness appropriate to the calling of a remnant community, can easily slide over into a loss of faith in the overarching purposes of God and a retreat from the obligations of Christian mission. In these conditions, the biblical language of lament, which is often neglected by the revivalists, can become the exclusive and normative language of worship. This seems to be precisely what happened to the post-exilic community in Israel. The psalms of lament, composed in times of deep anguish and confusion, became with the passing of the years the basis of a

---

23. The phrase is Andrew Walls's: 'A History of the Expansion of Christianity' Reconsidered (New Haven: Yale Divinity School Library, 1996), p. 29.

liturgical tradition which was increasingly divorced from reality and prevented those who were locked into it from recognizing the new things that God was about to do. This pessimistic spirituality was challenged by the living word of God:

> Why do you say, O Jacob,
> and complain, O Israel,
> 'My way is hidden from the LORD,
> my cause is disregarded by my God'? (Is. 40:27).

The recognition that the old theocratic institutions had come to an end, that there was indeed no way back to things as they had been, should have opened the way for the reception and embrace of the radically new thing that the LORD was bringing into being. Instead of this, many of the exiles were yielding to the temptations presented by an alien world, either by accepting Babylonian definitions of reality, and so sliding into a functional atheism, or by turning this 'liminal' stage into a permanent condition, and so becoming a withdrawn Jewish sect with nothing to offer the wider world. These are, I suggest, precisely the dangers facing 'sociological pessimists' today and both are paths that, if taken, would result in the extinction of biblical faith and hope in the Western world.

Revival and the emergence of world Christianity

The revivalist claim that we stand today on the cusp of the greatest spiritual awakening in history may appear bizarre when heard in the context of the Northern hemisphere, but it has far greater credibility when considered in the light of the surge of the Christian movement in the non-Western world. Any contemporary theology of the work of the Holy Spirit in revival must take account of spiritual movements in the South which, when considered carefully, do begin to look like 'great awakenings'. In sub-Saharan Africa, for example, a whole succession of charismatic preachers have had a huge impact over vast areas of the continent and have been instrumental in bringing thousands of people to faith in Jesus Christ. To cite one example almost at random, the wandering prophet-teacher William Wadé Harris trekked across vast areas of West Africa in the early twentieth century, summoning people to repentance, with results that parallel, if they do not surpass, the impact of George Whitefield in eighteenth-century Britain and America. This extraordinary ministry, like many others, remains a well-kept secret in the West.[24]

Similar phenomena can be discovered in China, where the growth of the Christian movement and its rootedness within Chinese society and culture has compelled Western sinologists to reassess earlier judgments concerning what was then believed to be the 'marginal' impact of Christianity in China.[25] The same thing can be said concerning Latin America, where the astonishing growth of an indigenous form of Pentecostalism has resulted in the dominant paradigm within the sociology of religion concerning the supposed inevitability of the process of secularization being challenged. The British sociologist of religion David Martin has testified to the manner in which his discovery of the explosion of Christianity in the Southern hemisphere compelled a re-evaluation of some of the basic assumptions governing sociological theory:

> Writing as one benevolently thrust into the epochal changes in contemporary Latin America, I can testify to the restrictive power of the governing [sociological] paradigms. Indeed, the epochal events concerned were well

---

24. On Wadé Harris, see Lamin Sanneh, *West African Christianity – The Religious Impact* (New York: Orbis Books, 1983), pp. 123–126; Elizabeth Isichei, *A History of Christianity in Africa* (Grand Rapids: Eerdmans; Lawrenceville, New Jersey: Africa World Press, 1995), pp. 284–286; Adrian Hastings, *A History of African Christianity – 1850–1975* (Cambridge: Cambridge University Press, 1979), pp. 67ff.

25. See Daniel H. Bays (ed.), *Christianity in China: From the Eighteenth Century to the Present* (Stanford: Stanford University Press, 1996).

nigh forbidden by the paradigm, and if they were not forbidden, their recognition was seriously occluded. Forty million Latin Americans just could not have been converted to a genuinely indigenous version of Pentecostal and evangelical faith.[26]

But, of course, they were. And if such empirical facts concerning world Christianity compel reassessment within secular, academic disciplines, they surely demand the most serious and sympathetic consideration by theologians and missiologists who need to wrestle with the implications of this still emerging, global Christianity. How does this extraordinary phenomenon fit within the analyses of both 'revivalist optimists' and 'sociological pessimists'? Of course, the kind of evaluative questions identified earlier in relation to Western claims concerning the appearance of revival also apply here, so that the surge in non-Western Christianity must be subject to biblical-theological evaluation and criticism. Nonetheless, the historian Mark Noll acknowledges that the growth of Christianity across so many cultural barriers at one time is historically unprecedented, and he concludes:

> Such multiple translations of the Christian faith at the same time in different parts of the globe can only appear chaotic, especially to those whose Christian experience is deeply rooted in the long Western appropriation of Christianity. What will become of the simultaneous translations of the Christian faith into so many of the world's cultures, God alone knows. But a long historical perspective can inspire considerable confidence.[27]

I conclude this chapter by returning to the typologies introduced earlier. I suggest that the evidence to which reference has just been

26. David Martin, 'Christian Foundations, Sociological Fundamentals', in Lesslie Francis (ed.), *Sociology, Theology and the Curriculum* (London: Cassell, 1999), p. 20.
27. Mark Noll, *Turning Points: Decisive Moments in the History of Christianity* (Leicester: IVP, 1997), p. 293.

made indicates that the revivalist optimists are not far wide of the mark when they propose that a spiritual movement of immense proportions is taking place around the world. It is worth noting here that the empirical evidence concerning the growth of non-Western churches compelled the American theologian Harvey Cox, who once advocated an extreme version of 'sociological pessimism', to radically reassess his earlier views. Cox, who in the 1960s famously (or perhaps, infamously) adapted theology to fit the paradigm of secularization we have just seen David Martin rejecting, now asserts that 'we are definitely in a period of renewed religious vitality, another "great awakening" if you will'.[28]

However, it would be a grave mistake for Christians in the West to imagine that they are somehow in a position to predict, far less to control, the precise shape and nature of the twenty-first century Christianity which is emerging with its centre of gravity firmly located among the poor peoples of the Southern hemisphere. As the churches in Africa, Latin America and Asia mature and seek for biblical answers to the pressing issues that arise in contexts characterized by poverty, sickness and oppression, their theologies and spiritualities are likely to take unpredictable forms and will pose questions for believers in the West that are likely to be profoundly challenging and disturbing. Thus, while the emergence of 'World Christianity' begins to look like a phenomenon of world historical importance, it would be deeply misleading to interpret it as nothing more than an extension across the globe of the kind of revivalist religion made in America and at home with Western cultural and economic values.

So far as the 'sociological pessimists' are concerned, I believe they are correct in observing that Western Christianity is in the throes of a massive paradigm shift and that, in this situation, it must renounce

28. Harvey Cox, *Fire From Heaven: The Rise of Pentecostal Sprituality and the Reshaping of Religion in the Twenty-First Century* (Reading, Mass.: Addison-Wesley Publishing, 1995), p. xvi. The 'early' Cox is represented by the famous work *The Secular City* (Harmondsworth: Penguin Books, 1965).

delusions of grandeur inherited from a now defunct Christendom and accept a genuinely missionary vocation in the context of the fragmented, hollowed-out cultures of Europe and North America. Whether the churches of the West can anticipate fresh movements of revival is a matter that lies within the sovereign purposes of God, but one is increasingly struck by the close analogy between our context at the heart of a global economy and that of the churches in Asia Minor described in Revelation chapters 2 and 3. As we saw in the previous chapter, these churches faced the temptations posed by the Roman empire and were promised the spiritual resources adequate to their calling in a deeply pagan and materialistic society, provided they were willing to pay the price of suffering even to the point of martyrdom.

No doubt times of great awakening bring much blessing, but the wilderness belongs to God as much as does the well-watered garden and sometimes the divine purpose in renewal involves the church in passing through the former rather than dwelling in the latter. God alone knows when the apostasy of the church reaches such a level that it requires purging through judgment. What is beyond dispute is that the gift of the Holy Spirit is promised to faithful Christians whatever the terrain through which they pass on their God-ordained pilgrimage. Whether in the desert or in the promised land, whether facing the great tribulation or standing on the edge of millennial glory, our task remains to listen to what the Spirit is saying to the churches today and, in fellowship with all who follow the Lamb of God, to overcome the many temptations and powers that would lead us into fateful compromise. Meantime, we anticipate the unfolding purposes of God with hope and joy, knowing that the One who declared to a bewildered and dispirited people, 'See, I am doing a new thing' (Isaiah 43:19) remains the Lord of our history. 'Revivalist optimists' and 'sociological pessimists' need to talk to each other, learn from their contrasting perspectives, and together await the coming of God's kingdom to which, it is to be hoped, they will respond with neither carnal triumphalism nor detached intellectualism, but with the awed worship of him who really does make all things new.

4   Islam, Christianity and Western values

For a few days before the destruction of the twin towers of the World Trade Center in New York and the Pentagon building in Washington, British newspapers carried brief reports of civil unrest in the city of Jos in Northern Nigeria. One report mentioned that the trouble had spread to the nearby town of Bukuru. However, these reports were very brief, indicating only that a number of people had been killed and that the Nigerian army had been ordered into the area to restore order.

On 11 September 2001, Jos disappeared from the coverage of the Western media, much as four passenger aircraft vanished from radar screens in America on that fateful day. Thereafter TV news bulletins were filled with horrifying images: passenger aircraft deliberately flown into buildings packed with civilians, people throwing themselves from windows above 100 storeys high to avoid incineration, and, most horrifying of all, the slow implosion of those towers with God alone knows how many people inside them. For days afterwards people in the United Kingdom could talk about little else, sharing a sense of bewilderment and incomprehension and a nagging fear that if fanatical terrorists were capable of this deed, they surely would stop at nothing in their attempt to destroy the Western world.

At first glance there might seem to be no connections between the events in America and those in Jos and Bukuru in Nigeria a few days earlier. However there are certain parallels which I wish to explore in this chapter. In the first place, there is a commonality of human suffering and loss. Clearly, the events on the Nigerian plateau cannot compare with those in America in terms of scale and the number of lives lost, but (contrary to those brief newspaper reports in Britain) it is clear that the loss and suffering resulting from the troubles in Jos was in fact considerable. Indeed, we may ask whether the differential coverage the Western media gives to events in the world suggests that human life is valued differently between the continents? One paragraph on an inside page for the deaths of hundreds of Nigerians compared to saturation coverage for weeks after the disaster in America. For Christians it is important to affirm that God makes no such distinctions; all human life is precious and the tears of widows and orphans matter to him, whether shed in New York or Jos, or by Christians or Muslims.

Second, the events in America and Nigeria have in common the fact that they shook people's self-confidence and stimulated serious thought and discussion on some fundamental issues. People not usually inclined to ask philosophical questions found themselves wondering what has happened to the world? In the West the disaster was followed by a remarkable outburst of discussion, reflected in newspaper articles of unusual depth and honesty. One newspaper somewhat sensationally devoted an issue to this discussion, calling it an 'Apocalypse Special'. Journalists used biblical terminology to suggest that we might indeed be facing the end of the world. In a rather more sober vein, writers tried to wrestle with the disturbing question as to what had created the depths of bitterness and human alienation that could make a deed as terrible as this one possible? The sheer magnitude of the horror in New York resulted in the resurfacing of the most fundamental concerns regarding human life as previously unchallenged axioms were shown to be inadequate, if not patently false.

Listening to conversations in Bukuru on the Nigerian plateau in the weeks after 11 September, it became evident that the troubles there had also triggered serious discussions. If a Nigerian state which prides itself on being the 'home of peace and tourism' (the official claim of the Plateau State) could erupt in violence of the kind witnessed in the opening years of the twenty-first century, then clearly something more than a nice slogan is needed to hold society together. Jos found itself asking the same kind of questions raised in divided cities around the world – cities like Sarejevo, Belfast, Bradford in Northern England, Jerusalem, Los Angeles and Johannesburg. Can people belonging to different cultures, different ethnic groups, and different faiths live together in a single state, or is separation the only way to survive? Is the model of the secular state now dead, destroyed by a rising tide of religious fundamentalisms, each insisting on their own unchallenged superiority and right to rule? And in Jos, as in America, the shock of these events prompted even deeper, existential questions concerning both Christian and human identity in a world riven by cultural and religious tensions.

However, the third parallel is both the most important and the most difficult to discuss. In the tragedies in America and Nigeria there was what we may call a Muslim connection. This inevitably gives rise to questions concerning the nature of Islam and, in particular, its relationship with the modern world. It is very important at this point to emphasize that the Muslim involvements in America and Nigeria were not of the same kind and we must notice the difference between the overt terrorism in New York and the far more complex situation in Jos.[1] Nonetheless, both events have exposed the

---

1. The complexity of the crisis triggered in Nigeria by the introduction of Sharia law on the part of Muslim-dominated northern states is recognized by Bee Debki in an account of an earlier outbreak of inter-communal violence in Kaduna in February 2000. While the author regards Sharia as unconstitutional,

fault lines which run between Islamic and Western (or Western-influ-
enced) cultures and it is precisely this aspect that I wish to explore
further.

Following the destruction of the World Trade Center and the
attack on the Pentagon building, both unarguably planned and
executed by Muslim terrorists, a wave of anti-Islamic feeling swept
through the Western world. In both Britain and America mosques
were defaced with hostile graffiti and Muslim women were spat
upon in the streets. Far-right political groups, whose leaders had
already been stoking the fires of anti-Islamic feelings, saw the
dastardly deeds of the terrorists as vindicating their view that
Muslims should never have been allowed to settle in Britain and
America in the first place. Estimates of the number of Muslims in
the United States vary considerably but the figure may exceed 5
million.[2] In large part this is due to immigration, but a significant
number of Afro-Americans, the descendants of African slaves who
were once firmly Christian, have converted to Islam to form a
black-Muslim community. On both sides of the Atlantic there is a
move within the majority populations to treat these Muslim communities as the new 'enemy within', raising the spectre of serious
social strife along this religio-cultural divide within the Western
democracies.

Meantime, political leaders, well aware of the dangers of internal
divisions as they planned the military response to the attack on
America, endeavoured to redirect the passions aroused by these

---

he recognizes that the troubles cannot be explained simply in terms of
religious conflict, but that ethnic and economic factors played an important
part in these tragic disturbances. *The Tragedy of Sharia – Kaduna Crisis From An
Eyewitness* (no publication details).

2. See Alan Neeley, 'Religious Pluralism: Threat or Opportunity for Mission?',
   in Paul Varo Martinson (ed.), *Mission at the Dawn of the Twenty-First Century:
   A Vision for the Church* (Minneapolis: Kirk House Publishers, 1999),
   p. 38.

events toward those perceived as the real culprits, the Muslim ex-
tremists, or fundamentalists, on the other side of the world. People
in the West found themselves in the unusual position of being
instructed by their leaders on the subject of religion. President
Bush and Prime Minister Blair announced that 'true Islam' is a
peaceful religion which supports modern, democratic ideals. Both
leaders appeared on TV surrounded by local Muslim representatives anxious to be seen and heard endorsing the assurances given
by the leaders of the Western world. The Muslims affirmed their
loyalty as British and American citizens and condemned the evil
acts of the madmen who had attacked New York and Washington.
President Bush, who had earlier made the crass mistake of describing the planned American response as a 'crusade', now made the
remarkable claim that all good Muslims everywhere 'share our
values'.

Islam and Western values

At one level President Bush's claim seems, frankly, absurd. If, as we
may suspect, the reference to 'our values' includes everything
intended by the phrase 'the American way of life' – including
unlimited individual freedoms – then it is impossible to imagine
Muslims adopting such values. The whole of Islamic history, not to
mention the teaching of the Qur'an, is against such a possibility. It
is not just a fanatical minority that reject the classic Western division of life into 'sacred' and 'secular' spheres and insist that the
worship of God must embrace the entirety of life; such convictions
are at the heart of a faith that refuses to put religion in a separate
box which isolates it from economic and political concerns.
Moreover, throughout its history, Islam has been a missionary faith
and has never been content (as, at times, has Christianity) to play
the role of chaplain to a society whose fundamental ethical values
originate from sources outside divine revelation. Rather, it has felt
impelled by a deep religious impulse to expand into non-Islamic

areas with the intention of bringing new peoples under the rule of divine law.[3]

In the light of Islam's fundamental beliefs therefore, it would be interesting to know just how Western Muslims react to the president's claim. It would be astonishing if, given a calmer atmosphere and the freedom to express their honest views, they failed to at least qualify their support for Western values. The plain fact is, as Craig Gay has recently said, that the fundamental presupposition 'embedded in modern institutions and habits of thought' is the assumption that 'even if God exists he is largely irrelevant to the real business of life'.[4] The title of the book from which this quotation is taken is *The Way of the (Modern) World. Or, Why It's Tempting To Live as if God Doesn't Exist.* If this is the ethos of the modern, Western world, then any Muslim who retains a living contact with his own, radically theistic, tradition is bound to at least qualify his support for the values of a culture governed by practical atheism.

It is this, I want to argue, that takes us to the heart of the clash between Islam and modernity. In a brilliant study of the relationship between Islam and the West, John Esposito observes that most Western perceptions of Islam have been shaped 'by a liberal secularism which fails to recognise that it too represents a worldview which, when assumed to be self-evident truth, can take the form of a "secular fundamentalism" . . . '. From this secular perspective, alternative paradigms, 'especially religious ones, are necessarily judged as abnormal, irrational, retrogressive'.[5]

---

3. See the classic studies of Kenneth Cragg, *The House of Islam* (Belmont, California: Dickenson Publishing, 1969); *The Call of the Minaret* (New York: Oxford University Press, 1964); *Muhammed and the Christian – A Question of Response* (London: Darton, Longman & Todd, 1984). See also Michael Nazir-Ali, *Frontiers in Christian–Muslim Encounter* (Oxford: Regnum Books, 1987).

4. Craig Gay, *The Way of the (Modern) World. Or, Why It's Tempting to Live As If God Doesn't Exist* (Grand Rapids: Eerdmans, 1998), p. 2.

5. John L. Esposito, *The Islamic Threat – Myth or Reality?*, 2nd ed. (New York:

In a postmodern, post-communist world increasingly dominated by a capitalist market economy with its base firmly located in the West, perhaps Islam's greatest challenge to America, and the feature that most causes secular intellectuals to dismiss it as an anachronistic hangover from an earlier age, is its insistence that economic theory and practice must be subject to divine law. Thus a Muslim scholar discussing the differences between the Western understanding of economics and that of Islam says that 'there is a radical difference between the vision of the good and successful life in the worldview of Islam and that of the capitalist or socialist world' (he was writing in 1983!). In the former, he says, the aim is to fulfil 'one's covenant with Allah' and to live life 'in terms of divine guidance as preparation for a more beautiful life awaiting mankind'. In other words, economic activity has both theistic and transcendent reference points; it is not an amoral activity governed by so-called scientific laws. The writer sees clearly that things are very different in the West where 'an essentially materialistic and earthly worldview' prevails.[6] It is precisely here that Islam presents an awkward, unwelcome and disturbing challenge, not only to Western secularists, but especially to Western Christians who have lived far too comfortably with a modernist world-view that excludes God from the public sphere of life. The question then becomes: do Christians share George Bush's values?

Oxford University Press, 1995), p. 249. This is by far the best book on Islam and modernity that I have come across. See also W. Montgomery Watt, *Islamic Fundamentalism and Modernity* (London: Routledge, 1988), and Norman Anderson, *Islam and the Modern World – A Christian Perspective* (Leicester: IVP, 1990).

6. Khalid M. Ishaque, 'The Islamic Approach to Economic Development', in John Esposito (ed.), *Voices of Resurgent Islam* (New York: Oxford University Press, 1983), p. 268.

Christianity and Western values

In 1915 a Chinese scholar named Ku Hing-ming returned from studies
in the West and composed a mock catechism intended to inform
Chinese young people about the nature of the Christianity he had
observed in America. It goes like this:

> Q Do you believe in God?
> A Yes, when I go to church.
>
> Q What do you believe when you aren't in church?
> A I believe in self-interest whatever happens.
>
> Q What is justification by faith?
> A To believe – each one for himself.
>
> Q What is justification by works?
> A To put money in one's pocket.
>
> Q What is heaven?
> A Heaven is to be able to live at Bubbling Well Road and to drive around in a
> large motor car.
>
> Q What is hell?
> A Hell is to fail.[7]

Clearly there is an element of mockery and perhaps of exaggera-
tion in this catechism. Nonetheless, it is consistent with the
reaction of non-Western peoples in their encounter with modernity over the past two hundred years, a reaction which discerns
that, despite the formal profession of Christianity in Europe and
America, the real religion at the centre of the culture is one of self-
interest and personal success. This same reaction can be detected in

---

7. Cited in Martin Jarrett-Kerr, *Patterns of Christian Acceptance: Individual
   Responses to the Missionary Impact, 1550–1950* (London: Oxford University Press,
   1972), p. 1. I have modified the catechism slightly in the interests of clarity.

the words of another Chinese scholar, Chee Pang Choong, a theologian based in Singapore and a visiting professor at the University of Beijing. He comments on a speech of President Clinton's delivered in 1988 in which, addressing immigrants into America, he advised his audience to 'honor our laws, embrace our culture [and] our most basic values'. With the courtesy characteristic of the Chinese, Professor Choong asks what exactly these 'basic values' might be. The question is pertinent when, as Choong observes, everything related to the sex scandals of this president had been openly discussed and relentlessly exposed to public gaze. In the eyes of the watching world – literally watching, courtesy of CNN Television which beamed its prurient coverage around the globe twenty-four hours every day – it seemed to be a Christian president on trial. Is it any wonder then that millions of non-Christians in Asia, and Muslims throughout the world, were left to draw their own conclusions concerning 'Western, Christian values'? Professor Choong asks President Clinton precisely the question we are raising with his successor in the Oval Office: 'Are there still any *basic* values left?'[8]

The response of evangelical Christians in Europe and America to this will be to point out that there is a clear distinction between genuine Christianity and the worldview and ethics which now govern the wider culture. This is, of course, a perfectly fair point, but the trouble is that for the past two hundred years Western Christianity has failed to make such a distinction. Indeed, it has frequently exulted in the convergence between the gospel and civilization. In fact, these two elements were often treated as almost equal components of the blessings which the West was called to bestow on the rest of the world through the agency of the missionary movement. It was widely believed that the deep spiritual needs of humankind, together with their supposed cultural poverty could be met through the spread

---

8. Chee Pang Choong, 'A Friendly Observer's View of North American Global Mission Responsibility Today', in Martinson, *Mission*, pp. 368–369.

of 'the gospel and civilization'. Consequently, it is now rather late in the day to begin the task of prising the gospel from the embrace of Western culture and non-Christians around the world can hardly be blamed if they experience difficulty in distinguishing between the two. Professor Choong comments, 'For years I have been trying very hard to convince my part of the world that it is a very serious mistake or misunderstanding to identify the West with Christianity without much qualification.' He observes that Asians continue to identify Christianity with the West and find it difficult to distinguish the two. And then he adds: 'It is not just an Asian issue, but a global one with profound implications for the mission and life of the church.'[9]

Back to Bukuru

So far the discussion has focused on the situation in the West, but I want to conclude by returning to the Nigerian context. When teaching a course on Christian mission I often use an acetate illustrating the church in Africa on which the Sahara, North Africa and parts of East Africa are shown to be areas with a Muslim majority population. The continent south of the Sahara, plus southern Sudan and Madagascar are shown as overwhelmingly Christian. But, between these two blocs, running from the north-east corner of Liberia, across the Sahel and snaking down into East Africa, is a bright red line which designates what the mapmaker describes as 'Areas of Tension'. Jos and Bukuru are located in the middle of this line. In other words, it is precisely here that two cultures meet and, as we now know, clash.

How should Christians respond in situations like this, where rival religious claims create massive social and political tensions? With regard to the controversy over the introduction of Sharia law by the northern Nigerian states, Sylvester Shikyil, a lecturer in the Law

---

9. Ibid., pp. 364–365.

faculty at Jos University, has argued very convincingly that this action violates the Nigerian constitution. He argues that Nigeria is design-edly a pluralist state which can only survive and prosper if 'all the major component parts . . . agree to adopt a system of governance that gives each of them a sense of being equitable stakeholders in the affairs of state'.[10]

The move toward the imposition of Sharia law appears to be a move in the opposite direction, toward the *de facto* establishment of one religion and the diminishing of the freedom of religion quite explicitly written into the Nigerian constitution. Therefore, Shikyil argues, the extension of Sharia must be resisted by all legal and con-stitutional means available because failure on this issue could seriously endanger the cohesion and stability of the nation.

Having said that, I want to ask what motivates Muslims in their desire to extend Sharia beyond the personal sphere (for which there is provision in the constitution) and into the realms of criminal and commercial law? One answer often given to a question like this is simply to state that Islam is a reactionary religion; it is by nature totalitarian and therefore represents humankind's past. Dr Shikyil himself appears to endorse this view when he describes Islam as 'a spent force in the emerging international system' and argues that Nigeria's future lies along the path of 'modernisation and progress'.[11] This view of Islam as irretrievably conservative and incapable of change is widely held and has articulate and powerful advocates both in Bukuru and New York.

With the greatest of respect, I want to suggest that it is a mistaken view. Of course Islam has many faces and there are deeply conserva-tive Muslims who claim to be the sole guardians of the purest traditions of their faith and seek to ensure that the community

10. Sylvester Shikyil, 'The 1999 Constitution and the Sharia Legal System In Nigeria'. *Research Bulletin of the Theological College of Northern Nigeria* 34 (October 2000), p. 29.

11. Ibid., p. 20.

is sealed off from contact with the wider, polluting world. But to treat such groups as representative of the religion as a whole and, on this basis, construct a model of normative Islam in terms of bigotry, intolerance and the propensity to violence ignores both the witness of sober history and the evidence of change within Islam today. John Esposito demonstrates that change, often rapid and disturbing change, is a reality within Islam and he says that the tendency to 'pit modern change against a fixed tradition' obscures the degrees of difference within modern Islam.[12]

Let us return, by way of example, to the many Muslims now living in the West whom we noted earlier. These are people who wish to affirm a double identity, both as faithful followers of Muhammad and as loyal citizens of modern, pluralist democracies. Obviously this involves tension as the Islamic traditions have to be related to, and reinterpreted within, the new pluralist setting in which political and religious freedoms, established against tyranny, are fundamental values. In such a setting religions change. For example, coercion in matters of belief must be renounced and in a pluralist society faith can only be commended by means of example, teaching and persuasion. Consequently in a close and sustained encounter with modernity, Islam is liable to become one religious option among others. In this respect it follows the path already taken by Christianity which once defended the divine right of kings and had its own brutal methods of compulsion when dealing with heretics and pagans. Just as Christianity has left behind its Christendom phase, so also Islam is challenged by democratic ideals and is likely to be compelled to discover ways of propagating its faith that are consonant with this context.

But to return to my question: what is the attraction of Sharia law for Nigerian Muslims? This is obviously a complex issue, but we should at least consider the reasons Muslims themselves actually give for supporting such a change. The preamble to the document introducing Sharia into the Nigerian state of Zamfara in 1999 says that this

---

12. Esposito, *The Islamic Threat*, p. 237.

action was intended to 'curb the high crime rate, moral decadence and anti-social behaviours now increasingly on the rise within the state'.[13] In other words, the declared motivation concerns the restraining of social evils and the encouragement of righteous behaviour within the state. Christians will of course have many questions about this, not least in relation to the Pauline insight that the law is a feeble instrument with which to address the problem of human wickedness. Nonetheless, it is surely important to understand, even to sympathize with, Muslim anxieties regarding the moral and social consequences of what is perceived to be a creeping secularization.

While driving from north to south in Nigeria one passes huge advertising hoardings. Most of these contain advertisements extolling the virtues of cigarette smoking. In one of them, young smiling Africans are sharing a packet of British-made cigarettes with the catch phrase across the bottom of the picture: BRINGS OUT THE LONDON IN YOU. It may be, as Dr Shikyil argues, that Nigeria's future lies along the path of growing modernization, but Christians, no less than Muslims, should be aware of the dangers that lie in wait along that path. Nothing could be more tragic than for the churches

---

13. See Shikyil, 'The 1999 Constitution', p. 32. It must be admitted that Muslim advocacy of Sharia often serves only to increase the anxiety of its opponents. For example, Dr Abdur Rahman Doi, professor of Islamic Law at Ahmadu Bello University, Zaria, argues convincingly that Western penal policies manifestly fail to arouse shame on the part of offenders and contribute toward the hardening of a criminal underclass. This is a valid observation which is reflected in new quests for forms of restorative justice in the Western world. However, Dr Doi then defends punishments such as amputations, stoning to death, and beheading on the grounds that they deter crime and prevent offenders 'from committing the same crime in the future'. The *logic* of the case is beyond cavil, but Muslims can hardly attack Western penal practices as inhumane and in the next breath defend such penalties. See A. Rahman Doi, *Non-Muslims Under Shariah* (Brentwood, Maryland: International Graphics, 1979), p. 13.

of Nigeria to simply repeat the terrible mistakes made by the Western churches in relation to modernity in the past two hundred years through an uncritical embrace of technology and the acceptance of a system of economics cut adrift from moral restraints and principles. Is it naive and unrealistic to suggest that serious discussions over these issues between Muslims and Christians might do much to take the heat out of the Sharia issue?

I come to a final question concerning Christianity in Northern Nigeria. Let me first say that there is a clear distinction in the New Testament between proselytism and conversion. The former existed before the coming of Christ and was the means by which Gentile enquirers were incorporated within the people of Israel. They were circumcised, baptized in water and taught the Torah. In other words they became, to all appearances, Jewish. The early church, faced with a massive influx of Gentiles, might have been expected to follow precisely this pattern. But, astonishingly, they did not; instead they struck out in a completely new and revolutionary direction. They decided that Gentile believers in Jesus 'should be left to find a lifestyle of their own within Hellenistic society under the guidance of the Holy Spirit'. In other words, apostolic Christianity did not demand conformity to a single cultural pattern but accepted a valid cultural pluralism from the start. This really was revolutionary. As Andrew Walls points out, the proselyte model would have produced devout Gentile believers but 'they would have had virtually no impact on their society; they would have effectively been taken out of that society'. Conversion, by contrast, meant that they turned toward Christ as Gentiles, as Greeks, and now sought to open up their culture to him. The result was that 'a truly Greek, truly Hellenistic type of Christianity was able to emerge'.[14]

My final question is a deceptively simple one: in the history of Christianity in Northern Nigeria have the churches approached the

---

14. Andrew Walls, 'The Mission of the Church Today in the Light of Global History', in Martinson, *Mission*, p. 387.

Muslim community on the basis of a 'proselyte model' or a 'conversion model'? Has the Muslim north understood the message of Christian evangelists who have frequently come from a different cultural background, one often associated with Westernization and modernization, to mean: to become a follower of *Isa* is to become like us? The question is crucial, because devout Muslims are unlikely ever to get close to the Jesus of the Gospels as long as the lifestyle of the evangelists and the worship of the churches makes him appear to be the destroyer of all that is treasured within their traditions.

Perhaps all of us, Christians in Bukuru, London and New York, need to reflect on the practice of the apostles in cross-cultural mission and seek the grace to take seriously today their extraordinary approach to conversion. In the process we may discover that we have more in common with Muslims than we ever dreamed possible and, by God's grace, Islam may at last have a chance to encounter the prophet *Isa* as he is set before us in the Gospels.

5   Fundamentalism and the Christian mission

In his acclaimed novel *Things Fall Apart* the Nigerian writer Chinua Achebe has given us an unforgettable description of the impact of Western culture, including missionary Christianity, on his own Igbo people in the rain-forests of Eastern Nigeria. With great insight Achebe describes two distinct approaches to the task of communicating the message of the Christian faith cross-culturally. The first is represented by a missionary who 'came to be respected by the clan, because he trod softly on its faith'. This missionary – 'Mr Brown' – made friends with traditional rulers and entered into serious dialogue with the guardians of Igbo tradition in order to gain an accurate knowledge of the beliefs and practices of his receptors. In a passage which should be required reading for Western Christians working in Africa, Achebe describes the long conversations between the missionary and a local religious specialist and concludes that, although neither of them 'succeeded in converting the other . . . they learnt more about their different beliefs'.[1]

---

1. Chinua Achebe, *Things Fall Apart* (London: Macmillan, 1965), p. 128.

In stark contrast to this, a later missionary is described as 'a very different kind of man'. He openly condemned his predecessor's policy of 'compromise and accommodation' and 'saw the world as a battlefield in which the children of light were locked into mortal conflict with the sons of darkness'. Here we encounter a model of mission characterized by intolerance, impatience and an unassailable conviction of personal and cultural superiority. Anticipating the disastrous consequences of this approach Achebe records, 'There was a saying in Umofia that as a man danced so the drums were beaten for him. Mr Smith danced a furious step and so the drums went mad.'[2]

It is significant that Achebe introduces these two very different missionaries in the sequence he does, with the culturally sensitive pioneer being replaced by a man with a much more rigid and doctrinaire approach to the cross-cultural communication of the gospel. The implication may be that at some point in the history of the missionary movement there was a significant theological shift, accompanied by changes in methodology, which resulted in the African traditional world being viewed in far more negative terms than had previously been the case. The actual experience of village people in traditional societies in Eastern Nigeria on the receiving end of Western missionary work may have reflected a paradigm shift in European missiology in which earlier views of non-Christian religions were eclipsed as a new breed of missionary came to assume that there was little or nothing of lasting value in primal cultures.

A historical perspective

It is worth stepping back for a moment to consider a broader historical perspective. In 1821 William Ward, a member of the famous 'Serampore triumvirate', wrote from India to a young man considering the possibility of missionary service and seeking advice on the

---

2. Ibid., p. 133.

most appropriate way to prepare for this. Ward suggested that, while the academic study of Hinduism and Buddhism had some value, there was no real alternative to actual encounter with people of other faiths. He counsels his correspondent to try and obtain first-hand information through personal contact with Hindus. Such knowledge gained through dialogue, Ward says, 'will be more correct than what you can find in books; and in gaining the relation from one on whom the system has made a strong impression, you will find matter for thought . . . which you could obtain by no other means'.[3]

Such advice anticipates by more than a century both the phenomenological study of religions and the fieldwork method which was later to become standard practice in the ethnographical studies undertaken by social anthropologists. If we are surprised to discover this degree of cultural sensitivity so early in the history of modern missions this may be the result of viewing the entire movement through lenses focused on much later developments. There is a great deal of evidence that, starting from a position fairly close to zero, many of the early missionaries exerted considerable efforts to gain an accurate understanding of non-Christian beliefs and treated the adherents of other religions with courtesy and respect. Despite rumblings from the churches in England, the Baptist printing press at Serampore was used by William Carey and his colleagues not only to print their translations of the Bible into vernacular languages, but also to produce versions of the sacred books of Hinduism and translations of the works of Confucius. This remarkable freedom (which scandalized African students when I drew attention to it in a Nigerian seminary recently) reflected Carey's determination to ensure that converts from Asian religions should cherish all that was good and noble in their indigenous cultural and religious traditions. At the same time, he took active steps to discourage the identification of the gospel with European civilization. The first generation of Baptist

---

3. William Ward, *Farewell Letters* (London: Westley and Davis, 1821), p. 242.

missionaries in India were quite clear that the purpose of God in mission is not 'changing of names, the dress, the food, and the innocent usages of mankind'; rather, it is to produce a transformation in human hearts and a radical change of values without isolating converts from their own, rich cultural heritage.

By the end of the nineteenth century however, this contextual approach was being eclipsed as very different motivations for mission came into prominence. By this time the missionary movement had become socially acceptable and drew its recruits from social strata very different from that of William Carey and his dissenting brothers. The powerful combination of the ideology of Empire and the impact of social-Darwinism led to a situation in which missionaries were able, to a greater or lesser degree, to incorporate the task of sharing the blessings of civilization with benighted native populations within their understanding of their missionary calling. In 1898 G. C. Lorrimer, preaching at the annual meetings of the Baptist Missionary Society, could claim, 'The united energies, faith and wealth of Great Britain and the United States, if intelligently directed, should be able in a few years to conquer heathen darkness . . .'. In words that would have horrified William Carey he went on to say, 'As the flags of the two living nations blend together, let us bathe them in the splendour of the cross of Christ; and as they move together about the globe, let us see to it that between them and over them ever gleams the cross.'[4]

Sentiments of this kind can be discovered in much of the missionary literature published prior to the First World War. In 1910, the year which witnessed the great Edinburgh Missionary Conference with its slogan 'The evangelization of the world in this generation', apologists for the movement noted that the attitude of Western governments toward missionary work was now wholly supportive. Eminent statesmen, it was observed, now publicly eulogize missionary effort and the church was poised to reap an unprecedented

---

4. G. C. Lorrimer, *Missionary Sermons 1812–1924* (London: Carey Kingsgate Press, n.d.), p. 182.

harvest across the globe. Clearly a missiology which could fuse evangelism with the global spread of Western civilization in such an uncritical manner was vulnerable to the Marxist charge that religion (in this case missionary Christianity) justifies and conceals the socio-political ambitions of the rich and powerful, providing ideological support for the colonial enterprise while leaving the poor and dispossessed defenceless.

It was just such a missiology which produced people like Achebe's 'Mr Smith' who presented Christianity and European culture as a total and indivisible package and preached conversion to Christ as demanding the repudiation of all traditional beliefs and practices. Achebe himself has reflected movingly on the way in which the education provided by missions for the African elite shaped his own sense of identity: 'I did not see myself as an African to begin with. I took sides with the white man against the savages.' Then, referring to the image of traditional Africa propagated in works like Conrad's *Heart of Darkness*, he says (with remarkable grace and restraint): 'But a time came when I reached the appropriate age and realised that these writers had pulled a fast one on me . . . That was when I said no, and realised that stories are not innocent; that they can be used to put you in the wrong crowd, in the party of the man who has come to dispossess you.'[5]

Contemporary criticisms of mission

Stories are not innocent. With the demise of modernity and growing suspicions that meta-narratives are to be distrusted, the missionary movement has been subjected to ever closer critical scrutiny. Some critics have tempered generally negative assessments with the recognition of noble and good intentions, even sometimes discovering

---

5. Chinua Achebe, 'African Literature as Restoration of Celebration', *Kunapipi* 12.2 (1990), p. 7.

evidence of heroism and altruism which challenged some of the pre-suppositions with which they had approached their research. However, some prominent critics have dismissed the whole movement as fundamentally misconceived and entirely negative in its consequences. Here the charges become much more serious: the missionaries are not simply fallible human beings, prone to mistakes, they are the active and willing agents of Westernization and are bent on the destruction of primitive cultures. Accusations of this kind reach their most extreme form when missionaries are accused of treating tribal peoples in a manner that justifies the charge of genocide. Norman Lewis, who might be called the 'prosecutor-in-chief', begins his book *The Missionaries: God against the Indians* with a passing reference to the work of the London Missionary Society in the Pacific region in the eighteenth century and then leaps across two centuries to indict the Wycliffe Bible Translators and the New Tribes Mission with direct responsibility for the elimination of traditional, aboriginal cultures in the rain-forests of South America. 'The great human tragedy of the missionary conquest of the Pacific', Lewis says, is being repeated now in all 'untouched parts of the world'.[6] By focusing on examples of questionable practice at the beginning and end of the history of the modern missionary movement, Lewis constructs a blanket condemnation which is breathtaking in its sweep. There are no nuances here, no different historical phases, nothing that redeems missions or even mitigates the charges levelled at them. In the language used by Achebe, there were no 'Browns' endeavouring to preserve, renew and revitalize traditional cultures; every man Jack (and Jill) in the missionary force was an iconoclastic 'Smith', wielding the Bible in fundamentalist fashion and displaying a spine-chilling fanaticism.

The same deeply negative image of missionaries in Latin America is found at the level of popular culture in movies like *At Play in the*

---

6. Norman Lewis, *The Missionaries: God Against The Indians* (London: Picador, 1998), p. 7.

Fields of the Lord. This film, released in 1991, parallels Lewis's approach at almost every point, suggesting that 'intrusions of North Americans on the soil and lives of indigenous peoples in other parts of the world' is both unwelcome and profoundly damaging in its consequences.[7] The fictional missionary organization depicted in this movie is called the 'New Fields Mission' – a thinly disguised reference to the NTM attacked with such vigour in the writings of Norman Lewis. As to the missionaries themselves, they are presented as caricatures of super-evangelizing and culturally insensitive fundamentalists.

More recently, similar charges have been levelled at modern missions in relation to the fomenting of a Hindu backlash against Christians in the remote forest areas of Gujarat in India. The Dangs tribal people, isolated and long neglected by the Indian government, have according to one commentator been fated to 'receive a quite disproportionate amount of attention from the missionaries of two rival fundamentalisms, one Christian, one Hindu'.[8] While the militant Hindu movements responsible for the enforced re-conversion of village peoples who have professed Christianity are subjected to critical scrutiny, the catalyst which led to a dangerous increase in tensions in this area was, it is claimed, 'a new wave of American-inspired Pentecostal missionaries – often south-Indian Christians who had received training and funding in the US'.[9] These missionaries are said to have been strongly motivated by the desire to see India's tribal peoples converted to Christ before the year AD 2000 since such 'people movements' on the subcontinent might presage a far more significant breakthrough, overcoming Hindu resistance to the gospel in an area perceived to be critical 'to the completion of the Great Commission'.

The missiology underlying this approach is one in which evangelism is regarded as the primary task of the church and non-Christian

7. Titus Leonard Pressler, 'At Play in the Fields of Missiology: Quincentennial Faces of Mission in the Films of Popular Culture', *Missiology* 34.4 (1996), p. 483.
8. William Dalrymple, 'Baptism By Fire', *Guardian Weekend*, 20 March 1999, p. 20.
9. Ibid., p. 22.

faiths are viewed in deeply negative terms. According to William Dalrymple, such evangelistic activity provoked the Hindu claim (clearly reminiscent of Achebe's criticism of mission quoted earlier) that conversion to Christianity is part of an 'international conspiracy' to divide India.

The charge laid against Christian missions is now clear. From Africa, South America and Asia come claims that missionaries have too often been guilty of insensitivity toward local cultures, they have made hasty and sweeping judgments concerning the religious beliefs of their receptors, and they were insufficiently self-critical, endorsing a Western, technological culture of which, whether consciously or not, they were representatives. Very frequently this critique is wedded to the pejorative use of the label 'fundamentalist', a term which has become synonymous with religious bigotry and obscurantism. In the remainder of this chapter I will seek to assess how far these claims are justified and to what extent it is true to say that a defective and socially divisive approach to mission can be correlated with Christian fundamentalism.

Missions and early fundamentalism

The emergence of the Fundamentalist movement in the United States in the early part of the twentieth century was related very closely to concerns regarding overseas mission. So central were these concerns to those who became identified as 'fundamentalists' that the work of mission can be described as 'a crucial factor in the emergence of fundamentalism as an organised movement'.[10] Evidence in support of this claim can be found in the famous series of paperback volumes which were eventually to provide the name

10. George Marsden, *Fundamentalism and American Culture – The Shaping of Twentieth Century Evangelicalism: 1870–1925* (New York: Oxford University Press, 1980), p. 167.

for this movement. *The Fundamentals*, issued as a 'Testimony to the Truth' between 1910 and 1915, contained numerous articles dealing with missions and evangelism and the final instalment was devoted entirely to this subject. In it Robert Speer claimed that 'the intention to conquer' is characteristic of the gospel. Christianity is an absolute faith and, as such, its attitude is 'not one of compromise, but one of conflict and of conquest. It proposes to displace the other religions.'[11] The background to this uncompromising statement was one in which a process of questioning and rethinking within the churches on the subject of missions gave rise to increasing anxiety on the part of evangelicals. At the very point at which the missionary movement appeared to have attained the peak of its influence (an awareness reflected in the quotations cited earlier in this chapter), the realization began to dawn that 'the non-Christian population of the world was growing faster than the number of converts'.[12] However heart-warming missionary accounts of conversions might be, the fact remained that Christianity was still essentially a Western faith with minimal impact in many parts of the globe. In addition, in the post-war years painful questions were raised concerning the 'Christian' character of Western culture. After the barbarity witnessed in the trenches of Europe, the assumption that 'civilization' was a blessing to be shared with the rest of the world was increasingly questioned by thoughtful people. Thus, the combination of the unanticipated resistance of non-Christian religions overseas and the growing indicators of secularization at home created a feeling of deepening crisis.

Conservative Christians reacted to this situation in a variety of ways. One response was to have significant consequences throughout the twentieth century and (as we shall see) remains important in relation to evangelical approaches to mission at the start of the third

11. Robert Speer, 'Foreign Missions or World-Wide Evangelism', *The Fundamentals* XII (Chicago Testimony Publishing, n.d.), p. 84.

12. Marsden, *Fundamentalism and American Culture*, p. 68.

millennium. Whereas an earlier generation, influenced by the post-millennial vision of Jonathan Edwards, anticipated great social changes as the result of mission, the fundamentalists developed a new missiology wedded to a far more pessimistic eschatology. The motivation for cross-cultural service in mission was now related to the passionate desire to complete the purposes of God in history and so hasten the return of Christ and the end of time. 'Bring back the King' became a new missionary slogan as the belief spread that the rapid completion of the 'Great Commission' might actually hasten the *parousia*. Marsden comments that, under the influence of the Keswick Convention, evangelicals were able to retain their optimism concerning the transformative power of the gospel by refocusing attention 'on the individual rather than on the culture'.[13] At the same time, the fusion of missiology and premillennial eschatology enabled the fundamentalists to retain mission as one of their distinctive marks while redefining its objectives and altering its motivation in ways that seemed appropriate in a shifting cultural context.

The abandonment of the grand missionary vision of the earlier evangelicals had already begun in the nineteenth century. John Nelson Darby poured scorn on what we might describe as Jonathan Edwards's theology of hope as early as 1840. Such optimism was 'delusive', Darby said, since all that can be expected in this world is a 'progress of evil'. By the end of the century key figures in mission on both sides of the Atlantic had come to propound premillennialism and to promote the idea that the early completion of the church's missionary obligation might actually accelerate the coming of the Lord and the end of this evil world. In England the enormously influential Grattan Guinness combined a passionate concern for mission with an absorbing interest in biblical prophecies to such an extent that the two subjects 'almost melted into one'. In America, A. B. Simpson encouraged the idea that the successful completion of the missionary mandate would hasten Christ's

13. Ibid., p. 101.

coming, even suggesting that by fulfilling the Great Commission 'the Bride may fix the date for the wedding of the Lamb'.[14]

Of course, this new missiology was underpinned by an appeal to biblical authority. While the so-called 'Great Commission' in Matthew 28:16–20 remained important as the ultimate basis for the churches' missionary calling, in practice other verses assumed great significance and were seen to possess huge motivational power. One such 'favoured text' was the Authorized Version translation of Matthew 24:14, which predicted the preaching of the gospel 'for a witness unto all nations' and then appeared to link this, almost as cause and effect, with the arresting promise, 'and then shall the end come'. Fundamentalist missionary thinkers read 2 Peter 3:12 (AV) in the same way: 'Looking for *and hasting unto* the coming of the day of God . . .'. What else could this mean but that it was possible for the church to speed up the prophetic clock? This fusion of mission with eschatology is captured in C. T. Studd's motto, 'To evangelize the world and have Christ back'.

This new missiology had a number of important consequences. As Klaus Fielder says, 'The conviction that it was possible to evangelize the world before Christ's return, or even to speed it, was a major reason why faith missions gave top priority to the unreached areas of the world.'[15] This is reflected in the names of the new wave of missionary organizations founded precisely in order to reach 'interior' regions neglected by the denominational missions which, seen from this perspective, had become institutionalized and immobile. We can trace the influence of this missiology into the second half of the twentieth century in the development of the concept of 'people groups', in the identification of the so-called 10/40 window, and in the plethora of plans and strategies designed to secure the complete evangelization of the earth before the dawn of the year AD 2000.

If it is easy to imagine how a vision like this could act as a positive

---

14. Klaus Fielder, *The Story of Faith Missions* (Oxford: Regnum Books, 1994), p. 277.

15. Ibid., p. 278.

stimulus for mission, it is not difficult to sense the dangers that lurk here. If the primary goal is the conversion of people who are defined as 'unreached' (which tends to mean the adherents of non-Christian faiths in countries shaped by centuries of adherence to traditional forms of religion), and if the linking of mission to eschatology creates pressure to reach this target in the shortest time possible, then mission can very quickly become a pragmatic affair best furthered by rational planning and efficient organization. David Bosch has observed that fundamentalist premillennialists have often seemed oddly at ease with the standards of the respectable American middle class way of life. Fundamentalist organizations (including missionary societies) 'were run in the same businesslike manner as those of their arch rivals, the proponents of the social gospel; nobody saw the incongruence in preaching withdrawal from the world while at the same time managing the church as if it were a secular corporation. Everybody worshipped at the shrine of the cult of efficiency.'[16]

Technology and temptation

At the beginning of the twenty-first century, in a postmodern culture transformed by the impact of new information technologies, the temptation to embrace every new scientific advance in an uncritical manner is vastly increased for Christians whose motivation in mission is related in a fundamental manner to the speed with which the task of worldwide evangelization can be completed. This explains the attractiveness of the media of mass communication for evangelicals. Radio and television opened up previously unknown possibilities of reaching vast audiences with the message of Christ; 'unreached' peoples could hear the gospel as sound waves penetrated physical and political barriers and the use of such media in mission-ary communication quickened the hope that, despite adverse social

---

16. David Bosch, *Transforming Mission* (New York: Orbis Books, 1991), pp. 318–319.

and religious conditions, global evangelization might be completed before the end of the twentieth century. Only later did it begin to become clear that the new technologies were not unmixed blessings, that an increase in the speed of communication might be obtained at the huge cost of a loss of depth, and that specific technological media possess the power to shape both messages and messengers in ways that could be profoundly harmful to the gospel of Jesus Christ.

Other examples might be given of the way in which the fundamentalist fusion of missiology with a particular eschatology has had negative consequences for the Christian mission. The literature produced by organizations such as the 'AD 2000' movement and the 'DAWN Strategy' (the acronym stands for Discipling A Whole Nation) breathes a 'can do' spirit based on the recognition of the power available to this generation of evangelicals through the gifts of modern technology. Thus, a consultation to discuss the completion of the Great Commission by AD 2000 is described in language which betrays a fascination with the power of technology. The meeting took place in a special 'Global Strategy Room' and as the doyen of the new science of 'missiometrics', David Barrett, used the latest audio-visual techniques to present his findings, it was 'like being on the navigation bridge of the *Enterprise* . . .'.[17] The mind-boggling lists of global plans, goals and strategies produced by this consultation suggests that, just as the original fundamentalists modelled their organizations on the pattern provided by the modern business corporation, so the present generation seem able to live comfortably within the structures and patterns dictated by postmodernity. Thus, amid 104 'Action Points' and 168 'AD 2000 Global Goals' the group meeting in this 'Star Trek' environment proposed to 'Initiate cooperation between the 42 million computers owned by Christians . . . Create a worldwide electronic Great Commission network . . . Maintain a

17. Jay Gary and Olgy Gary, *The Countdown Has Begun* (Rockville, Virginia: AD2000 Global Service Office, 1989), p. 28.

computerised calendar of all related events past and future.'[18]

At the biblical and theological level, the motivation underlying this fascination with modern technology remains that of accelerating the coming of Christ. In a book with the significant title *Then The End Will Come: Great News About The Great Commission* the creator of the so-called 'DAWN Strategy' writes, 'It is within our grasp to actually complete the Great Commission *and thereby pave the way for the return of the Lord.*'[19] This volume illustrates both the continuing attraction of the fundamentalist fusion of mission with premillennial eschatology and the great danger that this heightened sense of expectation can create what might be charitably called wishful thinking, bordering on self-deception. Thus, describing the current situation in England, Montgomery claims that the Church of England is in a state of revival, every major Protestant denomination in the country has adopted fundamentalist-style church-planting policies and God is 'anointing the Church in England to get back to its historic role as one of the leading missionary sending nations of the world'. British churches, he claims, could return to their 'former colonies' with a new vision and strategy for mission.[20]

If the sincere and passionate longing to prosecute the missionary task as quickly as possible in order to trigger the *parousia* can lead to such a skewed understanding of the situation in a European country – ignoring the realities of secularization, of the demise of Christendom, to say nothing of the end of the colonial era – how much greater might be the misinformation propagated with regard to nations shaped by Islam, Hinduism or Buddhism? The sincerity of those who teach this form of missiology is not here in question, but we are entitled to ask about the consequences of an approach that is so driven by the desire to achieve the maximum results in the

---

18. Ibid., p. 210.

19. Jim Montgomery, *Then The End Will Come: Great News About the Great Commission* (Pasadena: William Carey Library, 1997), p. xi (my emphasis).

20. Ibid., p. 54.

minimum of time that it divorces mission from serious theological reflection, downplays the reality of the impact of traditional religions on human cultures, and then seems happy to remarry missiology to Western technological and scientific know-how. It is precisely this form of mission that fuels the critical, secular reaction to which reference has been made earlier in this chapter.

Alan Neely, former Henry Luce Professor of Ecumenics and Mission at Princeton Theological Seminary, acknowledges that the deeply negative depiction of fundamentalist missionaries in the movie *At Play In The Fields of The Lord* is not entirely unfair since, he says, it 'reminded me of missionaries I knew . . . whose attitudes and practices I was pleased to see exposed'. Neely goes on to confess that he was not troubled 'that the weaknesses, mistakes, arrogance, pride, and sin that afflicts all of human beings, including us missionaries, were being divulged. How else could our human frailties be altered?'[21]

How else, we might add, can we be challenged to engage in serious biblical reflection on the adequacy of the theological foundations on which our missiology is built? In this respect I suggest that the fundamentalist fusion of mission with a particular eschatology needs to be challenged and dependence on a deeply unsatisfactory understanding of certain biblical texts, which almost placed the end of the ages in human hands, should be repudiated. Perhaps, as Samuel Escobar has suggested, we must today search not simply for tools that assist us in communicating a verbal message, but for 'a new style of missionary presence relevant to this moment in human history'. Escobar nominates Jesus' words in John 20:21 ('As the Father has sent me, I am sending you') as a key text for mission in the new world order since here 'we have not only a mandate for mission, but also a model of mission'.[22]

21. Alan Neely, 'Images: Mission and Missionaries in Contemporary Fiction and Cinema', *Missiology* 24.4 (October 1996), p. 454.

22. Samuel Escobar, 'Mission in the New World Order', *Prism* (December 1994), p. 17.

Mission and local cultures

No survey of the relationship between the Christian mission and fundamentalism would be complete without taking account of two very important perspectives which have come into prominence in recent studies. First, although a missiology of the type described above can do great damage in cross-cultural contexts, it is important to stress that hundreds, possibly thousands, of individual missionaries who might be identified (and would identify themselves) as, in a formal sense, 'fundamentalist' have nonetheless been women and men who have devoted themselves to imitating the example of Jesus Christ and have, in consequence, lived lives of humble and sacrificial service in cross-cultural situations around the world. Tribal peoples in Africa, South America and Asia facing various forms of oppression and experiencing the painful dislocations resulting from the impact of modernization have discovered a renewal of hope and a path leading toward cultural revitalization as the result of the work of such missionaries. Moreover, in contrast to social anthropologists, multinational business executives, TV crews and travel writers – all of whom return to the West after relatively brief cross-cultural sojourns to continue well-paid academic, commercial or literary careers – many missionaries have been committed to an immersion in local cultures which required living for years in remote village locations, entering deeply into local life and, crucially, taking the time and effort needed to master indigenous languages.

Their primary motivation in this respect was related to Christian communication and, in particular, to the translation of the Bible. Indeed, many of the missions charged by secular critics with the destruction of local cultures and religions have had the translation of the Bible into vernacular tongues as one of their central objectives. It is perhaps ironic that, whether intending this or not, missions have made an enormous contribution to the preservation of local cultures through the work of Bible translation. The sanctifying of the vernacular which this implied and the translation of the gospel story into local languages and idioms provided missionary receptors with a resource which enabled them to challenge Western cultural and political hegemony. The missionary movement thus played a key role in the emergence of genuine pluralism and multiculturalism.

This at least is the view of the African scholar Lamin Sanneh who has argued repeatedly and persuasively that the Christian belief in the essential translatability of the gospel has revolutionary implications for local, indigenous cultures. 'It is one of the great historical truths of our day', he says, 'that otherwise obscure tribes without a claim to cosmopolitan attainment, should find in indigenous particularity the sole grounds for appeal to international recognition.' Christian missions, often accused of being hostile to such recognition, actually preserved and renewed such cultures and, Sanneh says, 'the vernacular translations of missions . . . laid the basis for the modern nationalist phenomenon'.[23]

Second, as we have seen earlier in this book, there has been an unexpected surge in fundamentalist Christianity in almost all the places around the world which Western believers have been inclined in the past to identify as 'the mission fields'. It has been estimated that this form of Christianity now claims the allegiance of some 40 to 50 million people in Latin America, with a third of the population of Guatemala, 20% of the population of Chile and 15% of the Brazilian population in membership with the new Pentecostal churches. These figures are approximate, not least because the movement continues to spread like wildfire. The same phenomenon is found throughout the non-Western world, leading one observer to liken this 'vast, worldwide expansion of "third force" Christianity' to the sudden eruption in Europe of the Protestant Reformation.[24]

On the continent of Africa this development has taken everyone

---

23. Lamin Sanneh, *Encountering the West – Christianity and the Global Cultural Process: The African Dimension* (London: Marshall Pickering, 1993), p. 119.

24. Bernice Martin, 'From Pre- to Post-Modernity in Latin America: The Case of Pentecostalism', in Paul Heelas (ed.), *Religion, Modernity and Postmodernity* (Oxford: Blackwell, 1998), p. 106.

by surprise. Theologians whose attention had been focused upon the so-called African Independent Churches, which emerged a generation earlier in an attempt to incarnate the gospel in the context of traditional cultures, were unprepared for a new wave of Pentecostalism which appears to have little overt interest in the debates sparked by the earlier independents. Yet the enormous growth in this new stream in African Christianity has meant that it simply cannot be ignored since it is 'undoubtedly the salient sector of African Christianity today'.[25]

Although in a formal sense the Christianity being described here can be classified as 'fundamentalist' a number of careful analysts warn us of the great danger of misunderstanding which can result from such a description. Bernice Martin, for example, says that the term 'religious fundamentalism' has become so pejorative that its use in relation to the phenomenon of Pentecostal growth in South America skews analysis and prevents Western scholars from recognizing the positive achievements of this movement in a context of massive cultural change. She observes that the type of religious movement under discussion is occurring today throughout the Third World in places where a swift transition is taking place 'from *pre*modern to *post*modern conditions with barely any classically modernist phase intervening'.[26]

The transition from global capitalism to postmodernity is experienced by the poor in South America and Africa as a maelstrom of change and creates a context in which Pentecostalism is welcomed since it demonstrably provides 'an anchor in the face of dizzying new possibilities' and offers 'hope and lived solutions to problems arising out of structural conditions which it is beyond the power of individuals to alter'.[27] While believers in these churches would certainly affirm a fundamentalist doctrine of biblical inerrancy and

25. Paul Gifford, *African Christianity – Its Public Role* (London: Hurst, 1998), p. 33.

26. Martin, 'From Pre- to Post-Modernity', p. 108.

27. Ibid., p. 126.

would read Scripture in a highly literalist fashion, they do so 'less as a matter of settled principle than because they actually share the mental world of the writers of the New Testament'.[28] Martin traces the fascinating parallels between this form of non-Western Christianity and postmodernity and concludes: 'They have full post-modern credentials without the moral relativism' and may, therefore, be in a position 'to challenge postmodern culture not merely as little people from the margins but from within the heartlands of that culture itself'.[29]

I conclude with an illustration drawn from Africa which suggests that the careless use of the term 'fundamentalist' to describe the new wave of Christianity on that continent can be as misleading and mystifying there as it is in Latin America. The African preacher Mensah Otabil founded the International Central Gospel Church in Ghana in 1984 and preached a Pentecostal message with the promise of health, wealth and success. The church experienced remarkable growth and Otabil's preaching has begun to impact other parts of Africa. However, while continuing to take the authority of the Bible as a given, the cultural and socio-political situation in Africa in the postmodern era has provided a context within which this gifted preacher has begun to discover aspects of the biblical story that never struck the early fundamentalists in America as being significant. Thus, preaching on 1 Samuel 13:16–22, a passage that describes how the Israelites were oppressed by the Philistines and forced to use foreign blacksmiths, Otabil says,

> When I read this verse and I looked at the world and saw it happening plain on the world arena . . . I get amused when we talk of breaking the yoke of colonialism and still use the blacksmith called the IMF or World Bank to sharpen our tools . . . We see the sons and daughters of Africa roaming the streets of Europe and crying for crumbs from the master's table . . . In our

---

28. Ibid., p. 131.
29. Ibid., p. 142.

generation let us develop blacksmiths, people who will sharpen us, set us ablaze, equip us right here in our land.[30]

Here, as in Latin America, the belief structures of these churches may reflect a formal equivalence to the fundamentalism that originated in the West and was transmitted to the Third World through the agency of missions, but in the hands of local Christians wrestling with cultural and existential problems vastly different from those which obtained in the United States in the 1920s, these convictions become transformed in a dynamic way to offer hope to believers in the non-Western world and a searching challenge to their brothers and sisters in the West. In our unique historical situation, which is defined, as we have seen, by an entirely unprecedented multiple translation of the Christian faith simultaneously in different parts of the globe, we may be about to witness the fruits of the missionary movement in ways that could never have been anticipated. Through the seed of the word of God planted in the soils of diverse cultures around the globe, the new phenomenon of World Christianity comes to offer, in Lamin Sanneh's words, 'the promise of the new humanity for the twenty-first century and beyond'.[31]

---

30. Mensah Otabil, quoted in Gifford, *African Christianity*, p. 88. See also Otabil's studies under the title, *Beyond the Rivers of Ethiopia* (Accra: Altar International, 1992). This book has the significant subtitle *A Biblical Revelation on God's Purpose for the Black Race*.

31. Lamin Sanneh, *Religion and the Variety of Culture* (Leominster: Gracewing Publishers, 1996), p. 73.

6 Mission Africa – then and now

In 1991 the late David Bosch published a major study of the theology of mission entitled *Transforming Mission: Paradigm Shifts in the Theology of Mission.*[1] Bosch's work was to have enormous influence and has set the terms of contemporary discussion concerning the theology and practice of the Christian mission in the third millennium. Central to Bosch's analysis is the concept of 'paradigm change' which he took from the philosophy of science, where it had been developed in order to explain the manner in which scientific knowledge grew and developed over time. Previously it had been assumed that scientific findings accumulated gradually, so that as experiments and research findings grew in volume, so there was a constant increase in knowledge. However, the philosopher of science Thomas Kuhn challenged this model on the grounds that the history of science actually revealed a quite different pattern. While there were

---

1. David J. Bosch, *Transforming Mission: Paradigm Shifts in the Theology of Mission* (New York: Orbis Books, 1991).

long periods of what Kuhn calls 'normal science' during which knowledge increased within an agreed framework of theoretical understanding, Kuhn observed that there were also times of revolutionary change, when the entire structures of previous understanding were perceived to be inadequate in the light of new knowledge and so were replaced by a fresh paradigm. The catalyst for such radical change is the appearance of a visionary scientist, a Galileo, a Newton or an Einstein, who thinks beyond the existing theoretical framework. However, the representatives of that existing paradigm almost always resist the new insights, until eventually fresh findings attain such a level of credibility and explanatory power that they replace the old orthodoxy and become established as the new framework for understanding and ongoing research.

Bosch took this concept and applied it to the history of mission, arguing that there have been six distinct paradigms from the period of the apostles to the present. He explores each of these in detail, demonstrating their distinctive characteristics and showing how a variety of biblical texts had been used in each phase as justification and authority for each particular model of mission. According to Bosch, we are at present in the middle of the latest major paradigm shift in mission. Throughout the second half of the twentieth century, the received paradigm of mission has been crumbling and losing credibility, leaving Christians in the Western world in a time of transition in which they are compelled to search for new models which combine faithfulness to the authority of the Bible with relevance to the realities of a changed world.

The inherited model which is now losing its power is that of the era of 'modern missions' dating back to the emergence of Protestant missionary activity in the eighteenth century, extending through the Victorian period, during which there was a massive expansion of the missionary movement, and reaching its climax in the early twentieth century. Much could be said about the distinguishing features of this phase but what most concerns us here relates to the direction, or the flow, of Christian mission. From the very beginning of the modern era it was assumed that 'mission' was something done beyond the shores of Christian Europe in those parts of the world where Christ was not named. Thus, although there were undoubtedly great spiritual needs among the population of Britain in the eighteenth century, the movement that met those needs became known as the Great Awakening, a phrase that implies that what was needed here was not mission, but a revival that would make professing or nominal Christians into real believers. In the background here are obvious assumptions derived from 'Christendom', in particular the taken-for-granted view that Europe was blessed with a Christian culture.

The high-water mark of this understanding of mission is to be found toward the end of the Victorian period when Protestant missions, having passed beyond the phase in which they were suspected of being rather subversive institutions which might undermine British interests overseas, came to be respected and praised within wider society. In 1910 the great World Missionary Conference was held in Edinburgh in a spirit of optimism and confidence that the task of the evangelization of the world could be speedily completed. The conference divided the globe into two great blocs: one of these was designated by the phrase 'missionized areas', which meant Europe, North America, Australia and New Zealand, together with a tiny part of South Africa where 'civilization' was already established. Beyond this civilized sphere were regions 'not yet missionized', meaning everywhere else. It was taken for granted that the whole of the African continent belonged within the 'not yet missionized' areas.

Four years later, the terrible events in Europe which we have come to identify as the First World War shattered this picture. On the one hand, the untroubled assumptions concerning the Christian character of Western culture were called into question by the carnage which claimed the lives of so many young men. As we have seen in chapter 1, thoughtful analysts now began talking about 'the decline of Europe' and even about 'the end of humanity'. On the other hand, doubts began to surface concerning previously held assumptions regarding non-Western peoples and cultures and there was a new interest in non-Christian religions. Throughout the twentieth century the sense of self-doubt in the West increased as one horror was followed by another, resulting eventually in the collapse of both the modernist world-view based upon the eighteenth-century Enlightenment, and the Christendom understanding of the church and its mission, which shaped the thinking and practice of Western missions in significant ways.

Of course, existing paradigms do not disappear easily or quickly. It is important to realize that a period of transition is by definition a difficult and confusing time when two ways of understanding reality struggle with each other. We are, says Bosch, 'on the borderline between a paradigm that no longer satisfies and one that is, to a large extent, still amorphous and opaque'.[2] I like to illustrate this by reference to the not uncommon experience in traditional missionary deputation meetings when two slides get jammed together in the projector! The image on the screen is in glorious technicolour, but the detail will remain unclear until the first slide, which has already performed its function perfectly well, is removed.

The broad questions concerning the nature of the new and emerging paradigm of Christian mission have been discussed elsewhere,[3] but here I want to focus attention on the ways in which the continent of Africa has been perceived in modern missionary thinking and the challenges to such perceptions presented by the global context within which we now find ourselves.

---

2. Ibid., p. 366.

3. David Bosch's seminal work remains the key text on this subject. In addition, see F. J. Verstraelen (ed.), *Missiology: An Ecumenical Introduction – Texts and Contexts of Global Christianity* (Grand Rapids: Eerdmans, 1995); Wilbert Shenk, *Changing Frontiers of Mission* (New York: Orbis Books, 1999); James Engel and William Dyrness, *Changing the Mind of Missions: Where Have We Gone Wrong?* (Downers Grove: IVP, 2000); Samuel Escobar, *Changing Tides: Latin America and World Mission Today* (New York: Orbis Books, 2002); David Smith, *Mission After Christendom* (London: Darton, Longman & Todd, 2003).

Perceptions of Africa in the old paradigm of mission

I have mentioned the 1910 World Missionary Conference and it is significant that there was not a single representative from Africa present at Edinburgh. According to Andrew Walls, the main focus of attention and interest at this time was Asia rather than the African continent and, despite the impact of pioneers like David Livingtone and Mary Slessor, it was China and India that caught the imagination of the missionary movement and attracted its most gifted and able personnel.[4] We may wonder whether this was due to the prevailing perceptions of the peoples of Africa and of their religions, which, as the result of the influence of evolutionary theories of religion, were widely regarded as 'backward', in a way that the religions founded by Buddha or Confucius were not. The 'heavy artillery' of the missionary movement was best concentrated on the daunting task of confronting the ancient traditions of the East, while mission among more 'primitive' peoples in Africa might be left to the foot-soldiers of mission.

The dark continent

This leads us to an image of the African continent and its peoples to be found in countless missionary reports, hymns, and in the wider Victorian culture, that of the 'dark continent'. The term was used by the explorer H. M. Stanley who returned from his travels across the continent and classified the region as 'darkest Africa'. At one level this phrase may have referred simply to the element of mystery that seemed to pervade all things African, from the sheer geographical vastness of the place to the apparently exotic and alarming aspects of

---

4. Andrew F. Walls, 'African Christianity in the History of Religions', in Christopher Fyfe and Andrew Walls (eds.), *Christianity in Africa in the 1990s* (Edinburgh: Centre of African Studies, University of Edinburgh, 1996), p. 2. Andrew Walls expresses the matter as follows: 'it had long been the practice to send the missionaries with superior academic or intellectual credentials to India or China, leaving the celestial cannon fodder for Africa'.

its social and religious features. When the modern missionary movement began, huge areas of the interior of Africa were still completely unknown to Europeans and the era of the great explorations was only just beginning. It is not surprising then that the continent should provoke a sense of awe and wonder, especially when the incidence of disease and inhospitable climates appeared to protect the interior from outside encroachment and left its great secrets intact.

There was, however, a far more sinister aspect to the use of the term 'dark' in relation to Africa. Western perceptions were shaped by the conviction aleady alluded to above, that European civilization represented the summit of human achievement. As Darwin's theory of evolution came to be applied to the understanding of human history, so the peoples of Africa were frequently regarded as less developed than those of the West, whose peoples possessed the light of modern science. In its most extreme forms this categorization came to be expressed in explicitly racist terms. Evolutionary assumptions led to the distinguishing of 'higher' and 'lower' forms of life, and when such views were applied to the study of the history of religions, the conclusion was drawn that African beliefs and practices hardly counted as 'religion' at all. The term 'animism', invented to identify forms of religion in which belief in the pervasive presence of spiritual powers was central, came to be used at a popular level to describe the superstitious beliefs of peoples who were classified as 'savages'. So used, the term suggested that the vast majority of the peoples on the African continent were locked into magical world-views which lacked any sense of a transcendent God and were characterized by an unremitting sense of fear and despair. Such ideas undoubtedly influenced missionary perceptions of African religion and, in this respect, the older paradigm persists until today.

On the other hand, it should be pointed out that missionaries generally resisted overtly racist stereotypes, insisting that the biblical understanding of humankind required them to treat all peoples as bearers of the divine image and objects of the redemptive love of God in Jesus Christ. It is worth recalling that when the founder of the Salvation Army, William Booth, published his controversial study of social conditions in British cities and gave it the title *In Darkest England and The Way Out*, he was deliberately challenging racist models of humankind and subverting Stanley's depiction of the African continent. The darkness, Booth suggested, is not limited to distant lands which we classify as 'uncivilized'; it is found in the back alleys of the slums of London and, indeed, when the causes of the degradation of the poor are investigated, we shall have to conclude that it is also to be found in Whitehall and the City of London.

The wronged continent
Within the evangelical movement in Britain in the nineteenth century there was a deep and persistent awareness that a great wrong had been done to Africa and its peoples through the terrible trade in slaves that had blighted the continent. In a ten-year period at the end of the eighteenth century over 300,000 African slaves passed through the port of Liverpool *en route* to the Americas and the total number of Africans sold into slavery has been conservatively estimated at 20 million. At a time when we are urged to remember the Jewish holocaust in Europe, perhaps we might also recall this earlier, African holocaust and the havoc it brought to large areas of the world.

The evidence of Christian opposition to slavery can be found in the charter document of the modern missionary movement, William Carey's *Enquiry into the Obligation of Christians to Use Means for the Conversion of the Heathens* of 1792. When Carey comes to deal with the question as to how the voluntary society he proposes might be funded he makes this observation: 'Many persons have of late left off the use of *West-India sugar* on account of the iniquitous manner in which it is obtained.' Such people, he says, have 'cleansed their hands of blood' and the money so saved might now be donated to the new society.[5] In other words, missions could be supported

5. William Carey, *An Enquiry into the Obligations of Christians to use Means for the Conversion of the Heathens* (1792, repr. Didcot: Baptist Missionary Society, 1991), p. III.

through money resulting from an economic boycott begun as a protest against the evils of the slave trade. Throughout the nine-teenth century a sense of guilt over slavery was to play an important part in motivating missionary work in Africa. It was felt that European Christians had special obligations with respect to the peoples of this continent and that reparation for slavery might, in part, be made through sacrificial service designed to bring the healing gospel of Christ to Africa.

The contested continent

In the course of the modern era of missions the realization grew that Christians were not the only people with missionary interests in Africa. Islam had been viewed in many different ways in the nine-teenth century, including a tendency to dismiss it as an irrelevant and spent force. The future seemed to be so obviously in the hands of the West that a religion generally regarded as founded by an imposter need not be taken too seriously. However, as missions came into direct encounter with Islam across the Sudanic belt, the realization grew that Muslims had been very effective at propagating their faith and that they were motivated by a missionary fervour that could extend the house of Islam deep into sub-Saharan Africa. Islam was not tainted with the legacy of colonialism in the way that missionary Christianity could be, and it appeared to be able to present itself effectively as an African religion rather than as a foreign import. This clearly acted as a further incentive to mission in Africa and in places like Northern Nigeria large churches came into existence as a direct outcome of this awareness.

Africa was a contested continent in another sense. When the mis-sionary movement began, the European presence on the continent was minimal, with the exception of British control over the Cape Colony in the south. By the time of the Edinburgh Conference in 1910, the entire continent, with the significant exception of the ancient kingdom of Ethiopia, was under alien rule, shared between Portuguese, British, French, Belgian, German, Spanish and Italian colonial powers. The African scholar Lamin Sanneh observes that the

Western powers introduced, or rather imposed, an economic system on Africa 'whose chief beneficiary was the West itself'. The long-term consequence of these changes was to reduce African workers of local productive enterprises to 'the wretched of the earth'.[6] Thus was added a further great wrong done to the peoples of this continent, one which, as we shall see, has consequences that must be of particular concern for Christians committed to mission in Africa in the twenty-first century.

Africa and the emerging paradigm of mission

'Since 1910', says Andrew Walls, 'not only has the religious situation changed in Africa beyond recognition; there has also been a demographic transformation of the situation of Christianity in the world as a whole.'[7] The situation which existed at the time of the Edinburgh Conference has literally been turned upside down, so that 'the relative positions of European and African Christianity' have been reversed. Then, the normative shape of the Christian movement worldwide was determined by the theology and practice of the churches in its European heartlands; now the heartlands have shifted and Christianity in the twenty-first century will be shaped by the form it takes in the churches that continue to grow across the Southern hemisphere, and especially in Africa.

At this point it becomes obvious why the old paradigm of mission has broken down. During an extended visit to West Africa in 2002, I stood beside a missionary colleague on the platform of a church in Bukuru, in Northern Nigeria, where I had been asked to preach. The congregation exceeded a thousand people and faces peered through

6. Lamin Sanneh, *The Crown and the Turban* (Boulder, Colorado: Westview Press, 1997), p. 179. See too the same author's *West African Christianity – The Religious Impact* (New York: Orbis Books, 1983).
7. Walls, 'African Christianity in the History of Religions', p. 2.

every window. The worship was contextual and dynamic, including a series of thanksgivings for the birth of children, for a successful first year of marriage, and for grace given to a family in the year since their father had died. However, at one point we sang a hymn from the Sankey hymnbook which was a classic expression of the Victorian paradigm of mission, with a characteristic reference to the 'heathen far away'. At about the same moment my colleague and I became aware that we were both beginning to shake with laughter at the sheer incongruity of this song. And yet, perhaps sung in modern Africa it does make sense because, from the perspective of those churches, the heathen are now far away – in London, Birmingham and Glasgow.

The mental and spiritual adjustment that is required within the Western missionary movement to come to terms with the magnitude of the change that has occurred during the past century is challenging and difficult. It is not easy to accept that we have become marginal in relation to global Christianity and the habits of thought, practice and devotion cultivated by generations of devout believers throughout the modern era are not replaced without a struggle. Consequently, remnants of the old paradigm still linger on, reflected in language and attitudes that appear increasingly anachronistic today. Pius Wakatama from Zimbabwe reports how, as an African student in the United States some years ago, he encountered such misconceptions of modern Africa within the missionary community. He recounts attending a deputation meeting at which a missionary held up a traditional African musical instrument and, in response to a question, said, 'African music is just a lot of noise.' Wakatama confesses his anger that the unique and intricate structures of African music could be so misrepresented, but then he adds: 'This missionary knew nothing of African music although he had been in Africa for several years. I was consoled later, however, when I discovered that he knew nothing about Western music either.'[8]

---

8. Pius Wakatama, *Independence for the Third World Church: An African's Perspective on Missionary Work* (Downers Grove: IVP, 1976), p. 92.

Developments in African Christian theology

At this point, I want to ask how far the images of Africa already discussed might, despite all the changes to which reference has been
made, still be alive and at work today? For example, when the
Western media report events from this great continent the focus is
almost always on hunger, violence or natural disasters resulting in
the displacement of thousands of people. As a result, the dominant
image of Africa in Western popular consciousness is one of a continent in almost perpetual crisis, ravaged by the AIDS epidemic,
governed by megalomaniacs who bleed broken nations of their
wealth, and split apart by ethnic and tribal tensions that threaten yet
further genocidal conflicts. We may ask whether the stereotypical
Victorian concept of the 'dark continent' is still at work here, so that
the plight of Africa is blamed, at least by implication, on the assumed
backwardness of its people and attention is thus diverted from any
responsibility which the Western nations might have for the troubles.
It is not uncommon to come across statements like this one from a
Western 'expert' on Africa: 'Below the paper-thin veneer of civilization in Africa lurks a savagery that waits like a caged lion for an
opportunity to spring.'[9] In such statements the world is still being
divided into two great categories, with Africa as a hopeless case and
the West as the guardian and exemplar of all that is civilized and
decent.

This brings me to the second image discussed above, that of Africa
as the wronged continent. We may ask whether the wrongs done to
Africa in the past are not now being replicated in the deepest causes of
the seemingly insurmountable problems which the peoples of this
continent face in the age of economic globalization. We can be thankful that there appears to be a growing realization that the African
economic and social crisis requires special attention and that con-

---

9. Quoted by Bill Berkeley, *The Graves Are Not Yet Full* (New York: Basic Books,
2001), pp. 8–9.

certed action is needed on the part of the international community to address these problems. The danger is however, that solutions will be imposed which require the abandonment of African traditions, the further undermining of local cultures, and the incorporation of the nations of this continent within a global order which is dominated by the values and interests of the secularized nations of the West.

At this point we should consider the possible responses to this situation from the churches of Africa. As we have seen, the phenomenal growth of African Christianity means that the churches on this continent will play a key role in determining the normative shape of the Christian movement as a whole in the twenty-first century. In Andrew Walls's words, Africa now contains too many Christians to be regarded as being peripheral to the study of Christianity itself: 'And Africa may be the theatre in which some of the determinative new directions in Christian thought and activity are being taken.'[10] No one can predict exactly what this may mean, but we have already glimpsed one example of distinctively African theologizing in the work of Mensah Otabil at the close of the previous chapter. Prior to this however, in 1986 a group of 132 South African Evangelicals issued a remarkable statement in which they critiqued their own theology and practice in the light of their experience as Christian leaders in the context of a society split apart by the ideology of apartheid. While affirming their allegiance to the biblical gospel, these Christian leaders from Soweto concluded that the theology they had inherited from the missionary movement was 'blind to Western domination and exploitation of the peoples of the Third World' and belonged with a missiology in which blacks were still regarded as the 'mission field' while the whites are 'the bearers of truth and civilization'.[11] Insisting on the need to distinguish between winning people to Christ and advocating the capitalist system, they declared that 'unless

10. Walls, 'African Christianity in the History of Religions', p. 3.

11. The statement of 'Concerned Evangelicals' in Soweto was issued under the title, *Evangelical Witness in South Africa* (Oxford: Regnum Books, 1986), p. 31.

evangelicals broaden and deepen their conception of mission and evangelism their ministry is doomed in this country'.[12]

What, finally, about the third image mentioned above, that of the contested continent? The contest, we recall, was between Islam and Christianity and one important motivation for mission along the Sudanic belt and down into East Africa was the concern to halt the advance of Islam. This clearly remains an issue of considerable importance since, as we have seen in chapter 4, the fault line between Islamic cultures and those African cultures influenced by the West runs right across modern Africa. Without doubt this constitutes one of the great missionary challenges confronting Christianity on this continent, although in West African countries it often appears as though the political threat posed by Islam has overwhelmed a sense of missionary obligation toward Muslims.

However, I want to make the provocative suggestion that, important though the challenge of mission to Muslims undoubtedly is, it is in fact overshadowed by a yet greater challenge – that posed by the looming process of modernization and secularization which threatens every religious world-view on the continent. Indeed, as I suggest elsewhere in this book, the tensions between Muslims and Christians are not unrelated to this issue, with the former suspecting the latter of being simply the religious agents of Westernization. The tendency of churches to adopt Westernized patterns of behaviour, to worship in ways that suggest that reverence for God is not one of the fruits of the gospel, and to reduce the message of Christ to a religious product, all of this reinforces Muslim perceptions of Christianity as the religious carrier of a Western, secular modernity. We have seen how the modern missionary movement allied itself very closely with European culture and, assuming a highly technical culture to be consistent with Christianity, treated the task of civilizing backward peoples as an integral part of its mission. At the beginning of the twenty-first century, the question must be asked whether, by leaving

---

12. Ibid., p. 33.

the 'sacred' sphere isolated from the rest of life and sealing off the public realm from the challenge and influence of religious values, Western Christianity left the churches of Africa vulnerable to Islamic critique. Lamin Sanneh, who, as an African Christian convert from Islam has pondered these issues more than most, comments that it is doubtful whether 'religion as personal faith only is adequate to the contemporary global situation with its rising Islamic challenge'.[13]

So then, what is the shape of 'Mission Africa' in the twenty-first century? How does the still emerging paradigm of mission affect our perceptions of the African continent? Clearly, Western Christians should rejoice in the extraordinary growth of the churches in sub-Saharan Africa. To fail to do so, by retaining outdated images of the continent, is to fail to recognize precisely the manner in which God has been pleased to use and bless the labours of generations of dedicated missionaries. However, to revert to the illustration used earlier, it is now time to remove that particular slide from the projector in order that we may see the present situation clearly. When we do so, it immediately becomes evident that African Christianity is changing and developing as it seeks to work out what it means to be obedient to Christ in relation to the African past, and as it strives to relate its faith to the context of the modern, globalized world. Andrew Walls describes contemporary Africa as 'a bubbling cauldron of theological activity', and the outcome of this seems certain to involve a significant African contribution to the future of the World Christian movement, bringing blessing to the whole church as it wrestles with the task of mission in the postmodern age.

---

13. Sanneh, *The Crown and the Turban*, p. 211.

7   Mission beneath the cross of Christ

If, as I have suggested in chapter 3, the work of the Holy Spirit in revival and renewal has been of fundamental importance within the evangelical tradition, the theological heart of the movement can be found in its doctrine of the atonement. The cross of Christ has been the central theme of evangelical witness and preaching, so that historian David Bebbington can say that to make any other theme 'the fulcrum of a theological system was to take a step away from Evangelicalism'.[1]

It is clear however, both from Scripture and history that the symbol of the cross, whether this takes material or verbal forms, can be misused and distorted to such an extent that its original meaning is completely subverted. Within the apostolic period Paul already expresses anxiety concerning this possibility when he writes of the danger that the message of the Cross might be 'emptied of its power' (1 Cor. 1:17). The apostle envisages a situation in which the verbal

---

1. David Bebbington, *Evangelicalism in Modern Britain: A History from the 1730s to the 1980s* (London: Unwin Hyman, 1989), p. 15.

symbol, 'the cross', might remain central to preaching and worship and yet come to be understood and used in a manner that emptied it of its redemptive power, reducing it to a mere slogan which allowed, or even promoted, ideas and behaviour utterly at variance with the meaning of the gospel of Jesus Christ. It is this danger, and the challenge it poses for evangelical theology and mission, that I want to consider here.

Subverting the cross

Consider the words of the distinguished Jewish theologian Ignaz Maybaum in a collection of sermons, lectures and essays published under the title *The Face of God After Auschwitz*. The book was dedicated in loving memory of 'my Mother and my two sisters, three of the six million' and it includes a synagogue sermon entitled 'Auschwitz', in which he says:

> The Cross did not prevent the greatest carnage of history from happening; what happened, happened while the Cross was the sign of respectability, while the Star of David was the sign of the outcast; the cross was the smug symbol of a religion that lived in Concordat with Hitler.[2]

The justice and accuracy of Maybaum's accusation is beyond dispute as far as history is concerned. In April 1933 the Congress of 'German Christians' formulated a profession of faith which included the following statement: 'God has created me a German; Germanism is the gift of God. God wills it that I fight for Germany . . . For a German the church is the community of believers which is under the obligation to fight for a Christian Germany.'[3]

---

2. Ignaz Maybaum, *The Face of God After Auschwitz* (Amsterdam: Polak & van Gennep, 1965), p. 48.

3. Quoted in James Will, *The Universal God: Justice, Love and Peace in the Global Village* (Louisville, Kentucky: Westminster/John Knox Press, 1994), p. 190.

So complete was the capitulation of the 'German Christians' to the ideology of National Socialism that the cross not merely became a 'sign of respectability' but was actually incorporated within the swastika and used to affirm and sanctify the blasphemous claims of the Nazis. Little wonder then that Jewish thinkers like Maybaum should come to see the cross not as symbol of redemption, but rather as the sign of a religion that proved unable to resist or prevent the holocaust.[4]

The most comprehensive study of the reaction of the German churches to Nazism known to me is Ernst Christian Helmreich's *The German Churches Under Hitler: Background, Struggle and Epilogue* (Detroit: Wayne State University Press, 1979). At the conclusion of this massive study Helmreich writes (p. 463): 'It is apparent to all that the churches were slow to move, were beset by differences among the leaders and the ranks, and cannot be said to have won any glorious battles against Nazi activities and *Weltanschauung*'.

4. It is important to recall the distinction between the 'German Christians', who advocated an ethnic religion and endorsed the Concordat with Hitler, and the 'Confessing Church' which stood against such compromise and denounced it as apostasy. As we have seen, Dietrich Bonhoeffer played a crucial role in the confessing movement and in 1930, during a visit to the United States, he said: 'God has erected a strange, marvellous and wonderful sign in the world, where we could all find him – I mean the cross of Jesus Christ, the cross of the suffering love of God.' See Bonhoeffer, *No Rusty Swords: Letters, Lectures and Notes, 1928–1936, from the collected Works* (London: Collins / Fontana, 1970), p. 73. Interestingly, Bonhoeffer regarded the message of the cross as being counter-cultural not only in pre-war Germany, but also in the very different cultural context of the United States of America. He was worried by what appeared to be the inability of American theology to understand the meaning of 'criticism' by the Word of God. Anglo-Saxon Protestant believers needed to realize that God's criticism touches all religion, including the Christianity of the churches, and that 'God has founded his church beyond religion and beyond ethics' (*No Rusty Swords*, p. 113). This insight is extremely important and is, I suggest, of abiding relevance to Western Christianity as a whole.

At the same time, members of non-Christian religious traditions have often shown awareness that the use of the symbol of the cross in ways like those just described is a perversion of the gospel and a misrepresentation of Jesus Christ. The Jewish novelist Andre Schwarz-Bart seems to have recognized that such an ideological use of the cross involved a fundamental departure from the gospel. Indeed, so radical and monstrous was the subversion of the original meaning of Christ as to suggest a demonic influence at work within Christendom. In *The Last of the Just* he depicts a Jewish couple walking illegally through German-occupied Paris without their identifying Star of David, discussing the enigma of Christian hatred toward them and their kindred:

> 'Oh Ernie', Golda said, 'you know them: tell me why, why the Christians hate us the way they do. They seem nice enough when one can look at them without a star.'
>
> Ernie put his arm around her shoulders solemnly. 'It's very mysterious', he murmured in Yiddish, 'They don't exactly know why themselves. I've been in their churches and read their gospels. Do you know who the Christ was? A simple Jew like your father. A kind of *Hasid'*.
>
> Golda smiled gently: 'You're laughing at me'.
>
> 'No, no, believe me, and I bet they would have got on very well the two of them, because he was a really good Jew you know, sort of like the *Baal Shem Tov*: a merciful man, and gentle. The Christians say they love him, but I think they hate him without knowing it; so they take the cross by the other end and make a sword out of it, and strike us with it! You understand, Golda,' he cried, suddenly strangely excited, '*they take the cross and turn it round, they turn it round, my God . . .*'.[5]

What this quotation makes clear is that the true meaning of the Christian message, centred on the crucified Messiah, has often been

---

5. Quoted by C. A. Lamb, *Jesus Through Other Eyes: Christology in Multi-Faith Context* (Oxford: Latimer House, 1982), p. 29.

completely obscured and subverted in the actual experience of people in other traditions in contact with the historical phenomenon of the Christian religion. How many devout men and women belonging to other faiths have felt themselves, like the Jewish philosopher Martin Buber, attracted to Jesus Christ, yet repelled by the church? Near the end of his life, Buber confessed that he had come to believe that Jesus of Nazareth was the Messiah, but when asked why he had not become a baptized Christian, he replied that he found it impossible to abandon his own people, and then added: 'I cannot see what the Christian Church as an institution has to do with Jesus Christ.'[6]

And it is not only Jews who have reason to be nervous. The museum in Lahore in Pakistan houses a bronze statue of Queen Victoria which once stood at the major crossroads in the city. This relic of the age of colonialism remains undamaged, except for one thing – the orb in the queen's hand has had the cross surmounting it broken off. This act was in all probability prompted by the Muslim hatred of the cross, but Christopher Lamb asks whether it might not also be a warning 'that the cross cannot properly be used as the sign of empire, that human beings may not lord it over one another with the sign of the cross?'.[7]

Colonialism and the cross

The reference to the colonial era reminds us that the Nazis were far from alone in co-opting Christian symbols to support movements and ideologies utterly remote from the message of the crucified Messiah. Indeed, it is not difficult to find examples of such misuse by

6. Quoted from a letter of Max Warren in Graham Kings, *Christianity Connected: Hindus and Muslims in the Letters of Max Warren and Roger Hooker* (Zoetermeer: Boekcentrum, 2002).

7. Lamb, *Jesus Through Other Eyes*, p. 32.

evangelicals who believed themselves to be acting in a manner entirely consistent with a biblical vision of the church and its mission. This book opened with a reference to an evangelical author who, at the start of the twentieth century, rejoiced in the alliance between the missionary movement and imperial power. Anticipating the unhindered spread of Christian civilization across the world, he warned any 'non-Christian fanatics' in the colonies who might be foolish enough to contemplate action intended to hinder the onward march of the gospel that 'the strong arm' of 'Christian governments' would deal with them speedily and firmly. That is to say, the military power of the colonizers would ensure access for missions and would bring retribution on anyone foolish enough to offer physical resistance to the process of evangelization. The writer anticipated 'a general and determined engagement of the forces of Christendom for the worldwide proclamation of the Gospel.'[8] When we enquire what factors created such optimism, we discover that they were not theological or spiritual in nature, but were related to the political, economic and technological power of the Western world.

Sadly, this was no isolated case. As we saw earlier in chapter 5, a preacher at the annual meetings of the Baptist Missionary Society in 1898 could express untroubled confidence in the unfettered progress of Western culture-religion, using the symbol of the cross in support of a political project involving the conquest and suppression of other cultures. As America and Britain 'move across the globe', the preacher said, their flags will be 'bathed in the splendour of the Cross of Christ'.[9]

Prior to the cataclysm of the Great War, writers like these could treat Christianity and Western civilization as being indissolubly

8. J. I. Macdonald, *The Redeemer's Reign: Foreign Missions and the Second Advent* (London: Marshall & Scott, 1910), pp. 219–220.

9. G. C. Lorrimer, *Missionary Sermons 1812–1924* (London: Carey Kingsgate Press, no date), p. 210.

linked together. Such an approach to mission was, according to Samuel Escobar, merely one manifestation of 'imperial missiology', which undertakes Christian mission 'from a position of superiority: political, military, financial, technological'. According to Escobar, a direct line can be traced from the Iberian missions which linked the cross with the sword in the sixteenth century, through the Protestant European missions which combined Christianity and commerce in the nineteenth century, to the alliance between mission and information technologies at the close of the twentieth century.[10] In each case the meaning of the cross of Christ is grossly distorted and the message of the gospel is seriously compromised through its association with various forms of culture-religion.

It was evidence of this kind that led Søren Kierkegaard and, following him, Jacques Ellul to talk about the subversion of Christianity. Christendom, in Ellul's memorable phrase, effectively destroyed Christianity 'by making us all Christians'. By becoming the structural ideology of a particular society, Christianity ceased to be 'an explosive ferment calling everything into question in the name of the truth that is in Jesus Christ'.[11] Kierkegaard regarded the manner in which Christianity had been transformed into the opposite of what it is in the New Testament as evidence of a demonic attempt to destroy the gospel. In particular, he accused theologians, church leaders and pastors of destroying the very heart of the revelation of God in Christ by turning the cross into 'something like a child's hobby-horse and trumpet'. The Pauline warning had been ignored within Protestant Christianity, and the cross, retained as a visible liturgical and theological symbol, was 'emptied of its power'.

---

10. Samuel Escobar, 'Mission in the New World Order', *Prism* (December 1994), p. 17.

11. Jacques Ellul, *The Subversion of Christianity* (Grand Rapids: Eerdmans, 1986), p. 39.

The cross in a postmodern age

There are two factors at the beginning of the third millennium which compel us to give the most serious attention to the way in which the message of the cross has been perverted in the past and require us to engage in a serious, critical examination of our own theology and mission. In the first place, the postmodern suspicion of metanarratives and the consequent rejection of any project which aims to dominate humankind and impose a single belief-system is creating a generation of people who are profoundly suspicious of the practice of missions.

For example, the Australian social activist Dave Andrews surveys the history of Christian expansion and asks what he describes as the 'life and death question at the heart of the matter'. That is, 'Are the atrocities that are done in the name of Christianity true indicators of the nature of Christianity or not?'[12] Andrews's surprising answer is that coercion and violence, whether mental, spiritual or physical, seem to be integral to Christianity as we know it and that, therefore, 'we have everything to fear from the triumph of Christianity in the coming millennium'. He cites his own experience of the suppression of dissent and the exclusion of people who ask awkward questions within multinational, parachurch organizations as evidence that the fundamental attitudes and practices of Christendom remain alive and well.[13] I am in no position to know whether his account of work with particular organizations is accurate and fair, but in his profound alienation from modernist culture, his deep suspicion of an institutional Christianity that has been implicated in that project, and in his quest for what he calls 'a radical spirituality of compassion', his voice is *representative* of a generation of postmodern people who increasingly view institutional Christianity as an old religion which is past its sell-by date.

Second, if postmodern people in the West present one major

---

12. Dave Andrews, *Christi-Anarchy: Discovering a Radical Spirituality of Compassion* (Oxford: Lion Publishing, 1999), p. 48.

13. One chapter in Andrews's book bears the heading: 'Why? Wham!'

challenge to inherited Christendom models of church and mission, the phenomenon of globalization is giving voices to millions of people who have been on the receiving end of Western missionary activity. We have already heard the witness of Jewish people, but many other voices can now be heard protesting that the attitudes and practices of Christians have often appeared to be at odds with the One in whose name they came. Take, for example, the comments of the Japanese theologian Kosuke Koyama:

> Christianity has been busy planning mission strategy – this campaign and that crusade. People have become the object of evangelism since it is understood by Christians that they are 'automatically' living in the darkness, untrustworthy, wicked, adulterous and unsaved, while believers are 'automatically' living in the light, trustworthy, good, not lustful, and saved. The 'teacher complex' expresses itself in a 'crusade complex' [so that] Christianity has become a one-way-traffic religion.[14]

Koyama denounces such religion as an 'ugly monster' and describes it as completely at odds with the Prince of Peace who died on the cross. What is more, such religion is utterly alien to the Asian spirit, which explains why Western-style evangelism has made minimal impact on large parts of Asia despite the investment of huge financial and technological resources over a long period of time. What is needed, especially in countries like Japan, Thailand and India with their centuries-long traditions of humility, deference and compassion, is what Koyama calls the 'crucified mind'. That is to say, Christian witness can only become credible in Asia when it is channelled through people who exhibit self-denial, openness to 'the other' and a willingness to learn from them: 'If we have this mind people will see it. People are perceptive. They will ask the secret of this crucified mind. That is evangelism.'[15]

---

14. Kosuke Koyama, *No Handle on the Cross: An Asian Meditation on the Crucified Mind* (London: SCM Press, 1976), p. 52.

15. Ibid., p. 52.

Evangelicalism beneath the cross

Koyama's reference to the humbling of the mind by the experience of the cross highlights the central issue with which I am concerned here, namely, the need to allow the message of the crucified Redeemer to shape Christianity and Christians from the inside out. While the abuse of the visible symbol of the cross is relatively easy to identify and critique, I wish to ask whether verbal symbols, words or phrases, can mislead those who use them and erode the power of the gospel? Let me express this as plainly as possible in the form of a proposition: just as the material symbol of the cross can be abused in a manner that results in grotesque distortions of the Christian message, so also doctrinal formulations concerning the atonement provide no guarantee in themselves that those affirming them will live their lives beneath the shadow of the cross.

Indeed, as an evangelical who wishes to confess the centrality of the cross in discipleship, theology and mission, I find myself asking whether, despite all our protestations that the death of Christ lies at the heart of our understanding of the Gospel, we have not treated it in ways that have eroded its power and glory. How has it happened that people who speak with such conviction and assurance about the atonement often show so little evidence in daily life, or in interpersonal relationships, of a 'crucified mind'? Why are orthodox Christian churches and organizations, with belief in the atonement of Christ enshrined in doctrinal statements that are binding on their members, so often riven by ugly divisions resulting from human pride, anger and intolerance? And why is the message of the cross so often reduced to a private affair, a treasure confined to religious rituals, with no obvious connection to the agonies and spiritual hunger of the watching world?

In attempting to answer these questions, I want to recount a personal experience. Toward the end of the 1980s I went to West Africa to undertake four weeks of teaching in a quiet rural location amid the rain forests of the Niger Delta. Among the books I took with me on that trip was Jürgen Moltmann's *The Crucified God*. From the first page I was aware that I was encountering a theology of the cross unlike anything I had read before. Moltmann wrote that a concern with the cross and its meaning for the world had been 'the guiding light' in his work from the beginning and that this theme had become especially significant for him as he wrestled with profound questions concerning Christianity while a prisoner of war, behind barbed wire. A theology which did not speak about God in the sight of the One who was abandoned and crucified, Moltmann said, would have no relevance in such a context. Here the cross was being dealt with existentially, in the sense that this theology arose from the honest questions of an individual who had known what it meant to plumb the depths of loneliness and anguish so characteristic of people in the modern period. And yet, Moltmann immediately switched attention away from himself since, as he said, personal experiences are unimportant except in so far as they serve to focus all attention upon the one who has been experienced in them.[16]

Moltmann's work had a profound impact on me and, looking back over twenty years later, I think there were two reasons for this. First, I had discovered here what can be called a public theology of the cross. Of course, Moltmann addresses the church and its needs. Indeed, he speaks about the 'crisis of the church in present day society' and says that the critical choice before the people of God is not simply between assimilation with modern culture and retreat into the ghetto (as sociologists have been inclined to assume), but rather 'the crisis of its own existence as the church of the crucified Christ'.[17]

However, what struck me most powerfully was that Moltmann's theology was not done merely for internal consumption within the believing community, but was addressed to people in a suffering, meaningless and anguished world. The partners he chose to draw into conversation concerning the cross were not fellow-believers, but agnostic philosophers like Albert Camus and Jewish survivors from

---

16. Jürgen Moltmann, *The Crucified God: The Cross of Christ as the Foundation and Criticism of Christian Theology* (London: SCM Press, 1974), pp. 1–2.

17. Ibid., pp. 1–2.

the death camps, such as Elie Wiesel. I had myself been deeply moved and challenged by Albert Camus's works and by the unforgettable story that Wiesel had told of his terrible childhood experiences in Auschwitz and Buchenwald, and now to discover a theologian who took the questions raised by such people with utter seriousness and then showed how the message of the 'crucified God' related to them was a revelation to me.[18] I felt that I had discovered a missionary theology in which the cross ceased being the exclusive possession of the church and became something public, with redemptive and healing power far beyond the concerns of individual souls.

The second challenge of Moltmann's theology of the cross arises from the way in which it identifies the tension that exists between two aspects of theology: what can be called, on the one hand, its foundational authority, and on the other hand, its critical function. Moltmann showed how in the ancient world, the very mention of the cross in polite society was 'an offence against good manners'. In the cultured context of the search for the beautiful and the good 'the crucified Christ was not a valuable aesthetic symbol'. And yet, throughout the centuries the church had managed to empty the cross of its offence and transform it into a comforting, sanitized symbol of respectability. Consequently, Western Christianity, which once conquered the world, must now learn how to 'conquer its own forms when they become worldly'. For this to happen the churches would need to repudiate the idols of the Christian West and, in a truly reforming and revolutionary way 'remember the crucified God'.[19]

I mentioned that I read Moltmann's work for the first time while in West Africa. One Sunday I went to preach in a village church accompanied by a student from that area. After the service I was shown into

18. See Elie Wiesel, *Night* (Harmondsworth: Penguin Books, 1981); *From the Kingdom of Memory – Reminiscences* (New York: Schocken Books, 1990); and Albert Camus, *The Plague* (ET 1948, repr. Harmondsworth: Penguin Books, 1960); and *The Rebel* (ET 1952, repr. Harmondsworth: Penguin Books, 1971).

19. Moltmann, *The Crucified God*, p. 40.

a room in a small mud-and-thatch house and, while food was being prepared, my host gave me a photograph album and invited me to look through it. It appeared to contain the usual kind of snaps of him and his extended family taken around the village. Suddenly, as I turned a page I found myself staring at a photograph of a horribly mutilated and bloodstained body which was slumped against a stake. This ghastly picture, so out of place and completely unexpected, was deeply disturbing, but as I turned the pages I discovered a whole series of such photographs and suddenly realized that someone in this house, perhaps my student friend, had obviously attended one of the public executions that were then so popular in Nigeria and had kept a record of the event. Nothing I have ever experienced so brought home to me the horror and disgrace of the cross as I realized that my reaction of disgust and indignation at seeing those pictures was precisely the sort of emotions provoked by the death of Jesus among cultured Greeks and Romans. I now understood the 'offence' of the cross and the apparent absurdity of the apostolic claim that in this appalling, literally unspeakable event, God was 'reconciling the world to himself'. As Moltmann points out,

> The symbol of the cross in the church points to the God who was crucified not between two candles on an altar, but between two thieves in the place of the skull, where outcasts belong, outside the gates of the city . . . It is a symbol which therefore leads out of the church and out of religious longing into the fellowship of the oppressed and the abandoned. On the other hand, it is a symbol which calls the oppressed and the godless into the church and through the church into the fellowship of the crucified God.[20]

---

20. Ibid., p. 40. Of course, the distinction Moltmann makes between 'foundational' and 'critical' theology must be applied to his own theology. Indeed, he would expect this to be the case, so that his exposition of the Cross, like all other time- and culturally-conditioned interpretations, is subject to critical analysis in the light of the normative authority of the apostolic witness.

Evangelical and critical theology

What might it mean for evangelicals to take seriously the challenge that the church must 'conquer its own forms when they become worldly'? The subtitle of Moltmann's book is *The Cross of Christ as the Foundation and Criticism of Christian Theology* and I propose that the answer to the painful questions raised in this chapter may be discovered by exploring the tension between these two aspects of the doctrine of the cross. On the one hand, its foundational role is clear since this rests upon the constant and unambiguous affirmation of the apostles that 'no-one can lay any foundation other than . . . Jesus Christ' (1 Cor. 3:11). The apostolic witness to the death of Jesus constitutes the non-negotiable, normative basis of the Christian faith. At the same time, our doctrinal, interpretative and liturgical traditions must not themselves be invested with the authority that belongs uniquely to that apostolic witness. These traditions, however precious and revered, must not be granted foundational status because such a move would effectively inoculate them against criticism, making them sacrosanct, cordoned off and protected from scrutiny in the light of Calvary. On the contrary, they are to be subject to criticism and must, like ourselves, exist beneath the cross.

I wish to suggest that with the emergence of Christianity as a truly global, multi-cultural movement, the insights granted to Christian believers in cultural contexts very different from our own constitute a key resource in enabling us to develop a genuinely critical theology. For example, in traditional African contexts like the one referred to above, questions are often raised concerning the connection between the life of Jesus and his death on the cross. African theologians have frequently complained that the Christology they have inherited from the West jumps far too quickly from the cradle to the cross, leaping over the ministry of Jesus as though it was a mere interlude between the truly significant redemptive events. Yet, as we have seen in chapter 6, for Christians in rural Africa, facing pastoral issues arising from chronic sickness, spirit-possession and death, this leap across the life of Jesus removes from the Good News aspects of the apostolic witness concerning the nature of salvation that constitute vital pastoral and theological resources in the context of traditional, primal societies.[21]

Having been alerted to the possibility that we may have isolated the doctrine of the cross from the wider picture of God's redemptive love revealed in the life of Christ, we might wish to reflect on the possibility that, in a Western setting, this divorce has had the effect of obscuring the crucial importance of that life as both a gift to be received and an example to be followed. The New Testament is surely absolutely clear about this; central though Calvary and the empty tomb are in the apostolic message, they do not eclipse the memory of the beautiful life of Jesus, as though it could be left behind like the overture before the big symphony that everyone has really come to hear. On the contrary, the memory of the Word made flesh who lived among us 'full of grace and truth' suffuses the entire apostolic witness, shaping the life of the earliest Christian communities and being invoked in pastoral counsel again and again. The extraordinary fellowship of the first church in Jerusalem surely reflects a context in which the Sermon on the Mount had not yet suffered death by a thousand interpretations, and the repeated description of Christians in the Gentile world as the 'people of the Way' indicates that the apostolic insistence that the appropriation of the blessings of the cross was inseparable from entry into a new life marked by ethical and moral transformation was transmitted across

21. For example, the Nigerian Catholic theologian Kenneth Ennang, discussing the attractiveness of the African Independent Churches to members of the mission-founded churches, says that people discover within the AIC that the 'presentation of the saving work of Christ does not find a concentration on Good Friday alone'. Instead, Jesus is preached 'as a person full of sympathy for men in their sorrows and difficulties, here on the concrete plane of existence'. Kenneth Ennang, *Salvation in a Nigerian Background: Its Concept and Articulation among the Annang Independent Churches* (Berlin: Verlag von Dietrich Reimer, 1979), p. 334.

the cultural barrier between Jews and Gentiles. The perspective of the entire New Testament on this matter is summed up in the succinct statement of John: 'Whoever claims to live in him must walk as Jesus did' (1 John 2:6).

The answers to the questions raised earlier in this chapter now begin to emerge: it is simply not enough to affirm belief in the doctrine of the atonement if this is done in isolation from a living experience of Christ and a determination to walk in his way and be renewed by his Spirit. As the Lausanne Covenant affirmed, those who preach the cross must be marked by the cross; otherwise they will 'become a stumbling block to evangelism'.[22] I cannot do better than end this chapter with the trenchant words of René Padilla uttered at the Lausanne Congress in 1974:

> The New Testament knows nothing of a Gospel that makes a divorce between soteriology and ethics, between communion with God and communion with one's neighbor, between faith and works. The Cross is not only the negation of the validity of every human effort to gain God's favor by the works of the law; it is *also* the demand for a new quality of life characterized by love – the opposite of an individualistic life, centered on personal ambition, indifferent to the needs of others. *The significance of the Cross is both soteriological and ethical* . . . Just as the Word became man, so also love must become good works if it is to be intelligible to men.[23]

---

22. J. D. Douglas (ed.), *Let the Earth Hear His Voice* (Minneapolis: Worldwide Publications, 1975), p. 5.
23. Ibid., p. 1131.

8 Preaching Christ in a world of clashing civilizations

It is necessary to correct the tendency to base mission on a few selected texts from the New Testament. What has to be grasped is God's purpose for humankind as revealed in Scripture, and the missionary thrust of the whole history of salvation. This will throw new light on the nature of mission.

Samuel Escobar, *A Time for Mission*[1]

The biblical starting-point for the reflections in this final chapter is the seminal statement of Genesis 12:2–3:

'I will make you into a great nation and I will bless you;
I will make your name great, and you will be a blessing.
I will bless those who bless you, and whoever curses you I will curse;
and all peoples on earth will be blessed through you'.

---

1. Samuel Escobar, *A Time for Mission: The Challenge for Global Christianity* (Leicester: IVP, 2003), pp. 175–176.

The promise points toward a future which will bring blessing on a scale that is universal, embracing 'all peoples on earth'. Because of this it merits particular attention in our times when the world and its peoples appear to be increasingly divided and confused.

The title I have given this chapter contains an obvious reference to the widely read and controversial book by Samuel Huntington, *The Clash of Civilizations and the Remaking of the World Order* first published in 1996.[2] I bought a copy of this book in London in November 2001 and began reading it on a train bound for Oxford. At page 32 I read these words: 'People are always tempted to divide people into us and them, the in-group and the other, our civilization and those barbarians.' I looked up and suddenly noticed that scrawled across the back of the seat in front of me was a piece of anti-Islamic graffiti which declared: MUSLIMS WILL BE PUNISHED. WAIT! It is rare to receive such instant and chilling confirmation of the truth of a statement one has just read.

According to Huntington, the interactions between civilizations have passed through three historical phases. In the first of these, which lasted a very long time, there was minimal contact because, in the pre-modern world, different civilizations were separated by both time and space. The second phase began with the extension of the economic and political power of the West and resulted in a situation in which 'intercivilizational relations consisted of the subordination of other societies to Western civilization'.[3] However, we now find ourselves in Huntington's third phase in which the dominance of one civilization over all others is being replaced by 'intense, sustained, and multidirectional interactions among all civilizations'.[4]

While I strongly disagree with much that Huntington says in this book, it is difficult to contest the accuracy of the broad picture he

---

2. Samuel P. Huntington, *The Clash of Civilizations and the Remaking of the World Order* (London: Touchstone Books, 1998).

3. Ibid., pp. 50–51. Emphasis mine.

4. Ibid., pp. 66–67.

paints at this point. Indeed, what must be of great concern to us is the manner in which the new divisions he sees emerging within the human family impact the church and its mission. This was brought home to me very vividly recently with the discovery of an article by Ajith Fernando entitled 'A View from the Other Side of the Globe'. Writing after the first anniversary of the destruction of the Twin Towers and the attack on the Pentagon, the Sri Lankan Christian leader said: 'Perhaps there has never been a time during my lifetime when the opinions of the rest of the world have diverged so markedly from the opinions of the government of the USA.' Aware of the great dangers of precisely the kind of gap between North and South to which we have earlier referred, Fernando went on to say that the heart of the crisis is the sense among non-Western Christian leaders that their brothers and sisters in Europe and America seem unable 'to understand what is happening in the rest of the world'.[5] Fernando's bold and courageous plea to the church to 'divorce itself from the power of the West, which the rest of the world so much resents' needs to be heard by us, not least because it alerts us to the real danger that growing cultural and civilizational tensions in the world pose a threat to the unity of the church of Christ and the integrity and effectiveness of its mission.

This is the context within which I want to consider the seminal missionary text in Genesis 12:1–3. As I have said, the promise to Father Abram anticipates a universal blessing embracing all peoples. This obviously points us in the direction of the future and means that Abram, and all his sons and daughters in the faith, can travel hopefully through history. We now know that the world we see around us is not the world that will be; like Abram we travel through territory that is still in the possession of the Canaanites, but faith anticipates a time when not only this territory but the whole world will be transformed by God's mercy and saving grace. Put another way, we can

---

5. Ajith Fernando, 'A View from the Other Side of the World', *Connections: The Journal of the WEA Missions Commission* (February 2003), p. 83.

say that this text contains an eschatology – it puts a horizon in place that makes us a forward-looking people.

The Table of Nations

However, having said that, there is a danger that this perspective can prevent us from looking back to the chapters that immediately precede this text. In fact, I suspect that we have often read this statement as constituting such a radically new beginning, that we fail to recognize its connection with what has gone before. But surely the phrase 'all peoples on earth' clearly echoes the 'Table of Nations' in Genesis 10 which catalogues precisely the nations which 'spread out over the earth after the flood' (10:32). It is exactly these peoples and nations that are in view in the great promise given to the patriarch in our text. I want to dwell on the Table of Nations since I believe it offers vital theological resources for mission in a world of clashing civilizations.

Of course, between the promise to Father Abram in chapter 12 and the Table of Nations in chapter 10 stands the familiar story of the Tower of Babel in chapter 11 and our first question must be: how do these narratives relate to each other? There is a natural inclination to read them chronologically, so that the purely geographical description of the nations is followed by the account of their pride, rebellion and scattering across the earth which then necessitates the election of Abram. Read in this way, the 'primeval' history of the world in Genesis 1 – 11 concludes on a profoundly negative and depressing note with the nations hopelessly sunk in sin and under divine judgment. This then leads to the kind of radical contrast between the sphere of 'the world' and the realm of grace to which reference has already been made.

But there is a problem with reading the text in that way, because while the Babel story begins with the entire world sharing a common language which is then lost in the confusion of tongues, the earlier narrative explicitly and repeatedly says that each nation possessed 'its own language' (10:5, 20, 31). This suggests that these chapters should not be read as a running narrative but rather as parallel accounts stressing different but complementary truths concerning the human race. Clearly, the Babel story reveals the human tendency to act independently of God and to build the 'city of man' as an act of defiance against him. But chapter 10 shows the nations spreading across the world in obedience to the divine command in 9:1 and 9:18–19 and suggests that these peoples, in all their diversity of language and culture, are the objects of God's love and care.

I will not attempt to comment on the details of this remarkable chapter but we should notice, first, the unique character of this list of peoples. Claus Westermann observes that it has no parallel in ancient literature and Franz Delitzsch comments: 'Nowhere is there a survey of the relationship of peoples to each other comparable to this, so universal in its horizon and sweep, so utterly comprehensive in its intent.'[6] This is a vital aspect of the revelation contained in Genesis 1–11 because, in our context of the 'clash of civilizations', it serves as a reminder that these foundational chapters must lead us to oppose the kind of ethnocentrism that exalts one nation or culture and denigrates all others.

What is of supreme importance for us, however, is that this remarkable description of the nations of the world forms the context within which Abram is called to leave his country as the first step on the long pilgrimage which will end with these very nations being blessed. That is to say, the divine election recorded in chapter 12 is not a withdrawal from the world of the nations, as though God has given up on them and now settles for the more limited objective of saving one particular people. For sure, Genesis 12 records a new beginning, but this can only be appreciated when it is set within the context provided by what has gone before. The election of Israel does not imply

---

6. See Claus Westermann, *Genesis 1–11: A Commentary* (Minneapolis: Augsburg Publishing, 1984), p. 501. The quotation from Delitzsch is cited by Westermann on p. 528 of this commentary.

the rejection of the nations but, on the contrary, is the means by which grace and salvation will extend to this wider world which God so clearly loves. As Johannes Blauw puts it: 'The call of Abraham must be seen in the light of God's revelation to the nations . . . The act of election coincides with the promise or prospect of blessing for the nations.' He goes on to say: 'The purpose of election is service, and when the service is withheld the election loses its meaning.'[7]

I want to notice, second, the way in which this primal vision of the blessing of the nations resurfaces throughout the Old Testament. It is of course true that the nations are often seen as a threat to the purity of Israel's faith and that the vision of the day when they will come to share in the worship of God is often lost. However, the influence of these primal narratives can be seen again and again throughout the history of Israel, especially following the exile when those who were taken into captivity were compelled to ask new questions concerning the relationship between the covenant faith and the mighty empires which they now encountered in a most direct way.

Consider a passage that seems especially important at the present time. Isaiah anticipates the day when all nations will stream to Zion to be instructed in the way of God and, as a result, will experience a reconciliation that will bring a final and complete end to the arms industry (Is. 2:1–5). In the previous chapter the prophet had denounced Israel because she had forgotten the purpose of divine election and now he summons those willing to hear the word of God to 'walk in the light of the LORD' (2:5). That is to say, they are to allow the vision of God's future, which brings all nations into the kingdom, to shape their present behaviour. That future still lies at a distance from the present, a promise for the last days, but for Isaiah as for Abram, faith sees this as the ultimate reality, in contrast to the existing state of affairs which is based on tragic delusions and superstitions.

---

7. Johannes Blauw, *The Missionary Nature of the Church* (London: Lutterworth Press, 1962), p. 22.

There are places in the Old Testament where the ancient hope that all nations will come to worship God breaks through with such clarity and boldness as to take us completely by surprise. Indeed, I sometimes wonder whether a distorted understanding of divine election has not skewed our perspective so that we read the Bible in a way that filters out the evidence of the freedom and liberality of divine grace. For example, Daniel 4 introduces a pagan ruler who strides across history like a colossus who testifies to all nations (Daniel 4:1) that he has been humbled and brought to worship the 'King of heaven' who does what is 'right' and whose 'ways are just' (Daniel 4:37). It is almost as though the two parallel lines that began in Genesis 10 and 11 converge and meet at this point, as the proud ruler of Babylon, who so epitomizes the godless spirit of those who in Genesis 11 are determined to 'make a name' for themselves, is converted to the worship of God and so becomes a kind of first-fruit of those peoples listed in the Table of Nations as the objects of divine concern and grace.

Or consider the extraordinary revelation contained in Psalm 87, which begins with a conventional description of the glories of Zion and is then suddenly and dramatically transformed by the statement that God keeps a register of the peoples in which nations such as Egypt, Babylon, Philistia, Tyre and Ethiopia are recorded among those 'who acknowledge me' (Ps. 87:4). It is worth quoting at some length the words of the commentator Artur Weiser on this remarkable psalm:

> It is as if the whole world had agreed to meet in this place. They have come from the Nile and the Euphrates, from the land of the Philistines and of the Phoenicians, and even black figures from distant Ethiopia are not absent from this gathering of the nations in the house of God on Mount Zion. However much they may differ from each other in language and appearance, they are all united in one *faith,* believing the *one* God whom they jointly profess.'[8]

---

8. Artur Weiser, *The Psalms – A Commentary* (London: SCM Press, 1962), p. 580. On the assumption that the context of this psalm is to be found in the experience of the exile, other commentators suggest that what is in view here is not

I want to turn, third, to the way in which the Old Testament understanding of the nations is picked up and developed in the New Testament. As we know very well this motif is present in many key texts, especially those related to the missionary calling of the people of God. The command of the risen Christ is to make disciples of all nations (Matt. 28:19). In Acts 2 those parallel lines from Genesis again converge as the confusion of tongues at Babel is reversed among a crowd gathered from every nation under heaven (Acts 2:5–8). The Apocalypse anticipates the time when a numberless multitude 'from every nation, tribe, people and language' will stand before the throne of God' (Rev. 7:9).

However, I want to observe the way in which the primal narratives in Genesis 10 – 11 operate in the life and ministry of a missionary who finds himself facing an audience with decidedly ethnocentric tendencies. I refer, of course, to Paul's message on Mars Hill in Athens recorded in Acts 17. Throughout this story there are echoes of the two chapters in Genesis with which we have been concerned. For example, when the Epicurean and Stoic philosophers who make up the apostle's audience ask, 'What is this babbler trying to say?' (Acts

---

the conversion of the nations but the scattering of the people of God among them. Thus, Hans-Joachim Kraus says that God here lists 'the nations among which Israel is dispersed' and affirms that 'Zion is the mother of all Israelites living in the dispersion'. Hans-Joachim Kraus, *Psalms 60 – 150 – A Commentary* (Minneapolis: Augsburg Publishing, 1989), p. 188. However, it seems clear that the 'register' being kept by God relates to the peoples rather than to some group among them, and this fits well with the view of the nations we have traced through the Old Testament. As Weiser says (pp. 582–583), this is a visionary picture, 'conceived with prophetic power' in which the psalmist sees 'the great people of God which no longer comprises only Israel but embraces all the nations'. To this must be added the fact that the psalms frequently affirm the universal sovereignty of God and anticipate the time when this will be recognized by all nations. For example, Psalm 47 ends (v. 9) with the prediction that the 'nobles of the nations' will assemble 'as the people of the God of Abraham' since 'the kings of the earth belong to God'.

17:18) they are making a derogatory reference to his ideas and language and imply that he belongs to a category of people who are without civilization. For these proud Greeks there is but one, universal language and culture outside of which nothing but incoherent babble can be heard. The spirit of those who built the tower of Babel and attempted to ensure that a common speech dominated the whole earth was alive and well on Mars Hill.

But if the hubris of the Greeks in Athens recalls the story of Babel, Paul's response goes back beyond this to the Table of Nations:

'The God who made the world and everything in it is Lord of heaven and earth and does not live in temples built by hands . . . From one man he made every nation of men, that they should inhabit the whole earth; and he determined the times set for them and the exact places where they should live.' (Acts 17:24–26)

In affirming a biblical doctrine of creation and providence, Paul denies the arrogant Greek claim to linguistic and cultural superiority while, at the same time, insisting that the variety of cultures is willed by God and fulfils his purpose for the world. Indeed, he goes on to say that God determined the places and times that nations should live 'so that men would seek him and perhaps reach out for him and find him' (Acts 17:27). This Pauline anthropology is rooted in the early narratives of Genesis and clearly echoes the Table of the Nations with its insistence that God loves all peoples and wills their salvation.

So then, where does all of this leave us in relation to the challenge we face today as a missionary people in a time when civilizations are again in conflict? The problem for Western Christians today is that, in contrast to the situation faced by Paul, we belong to a culture that is strong and powerful and is tempted to view itself as superior among the nations. We are the 'new Greeks' with a tendency to look out on a confusing world of 'babblers'. Even though as Christians we distance ourselves from such attitudes, we cannot change the fact that we belong to a dominant and immensely powerful culture which possesses unprecedented economic, political and military strength.

In such a context the question to be asked is how we can do mission from such a position? This is the question being asked today by increasing numbers of believers from the Southern hemisphere who would agree with the words of Ajith Fernando written in 2002, before American and British forces invaded Iraq:

> Paul said that he became weak to reach the weak (1 Cor. 9:22). The Muslims see themselves as threatened by the strength of the West. I think that if we are to reach them with the Gospel we will have to identify with their sense of weakness. We will have to become weak ourselves. If they see the Christians as strong people coming to hit them, they will hate us and oppose our Gospel even more. This is why it may be necessary for the church to divorce itself from the power of the West, which most of the rest of the world resents. In a similar vein, it is necessary for the church to divorce itself from statements like 'We are the greatest nation on earth' because our religion tells us, 'In humility consider others better than yourselves' (Phil. 2:3). These are vital issues that churches in the West need to be thinking about if they are to be involved in missions.[9]

The Tower of Babel

I want to turn now to the second of the two chapters in Genesis which, as I suggested earlier, must be read as parallel accounts of the condition of the human race. If the Table of Nations reveals God's grace at work in the world and affirms that all people belong ultimately to one human family, a much darker picture emerges in chapter 11. This suggests that while we need the reminder provided by chapter 10 that God loves the nations and is at work among them, the story of the Tower of Babel prevents us from reaching a secular humanist conclusion in which the reality of sin is denied and the need for redemption is removed. Indeed, this could be precisely the

---

9. Fernando, 'A View from the Other Side of the World', p. 85.

reason that these two chapters appear in the order that they do: had the story of the Tower of Babel come first, followed by the positive picture of the scattered nations, we might well conclude that the peoples of the world were living 'in brotherly concord, fulfilling God's command to fill the earth and subdue it'.[10] Alas, as we shall see, that is not the case.

Consider first, the context of the building of Babel. We are told that 'the whole world' possessed a common language and culture. This is not an evil thing in and of itself because the Bible anticipates a time when the new humankind will be so united within the kingdom of God. However, under the conditions created by the fall into sin, this unity of language (or the aspiration to achieve it) becomes a dangerous thing because it is used to build a society independent of the Creator and freed from the constraints of his Word.

There is also significance in the fact that as people moved eastwards and discovered 'a plain in Shinar' they are explicitly said to have 'settled there'. There is something ominous about this settling down and it stands in clear contrast to the summons to Abram in the next chapter to leave his country, people and household (12:1). What is suspect here is not the desire for a place that can be called 'home': the previous chapter validates local cultures and specific ethnic and cultural identities. Once again, the problem is that in a fallen world people 'settle' in the sense that they create an environment which eliminates reminders of the reality of the human condition. They settle in an absolute sense, attempting to turn this fallen and tragic world into something permanent, suppressing the fact of suffering and death in a substitute paradise from which God is excluded.

Of course, the theme of pilgrimage, of a people always mobile and moving on, is prominent throughout the Bible and is important to the understanding of the Christian mission. In a fascinating study of Genesis 1 – 11 from an Afro-Asiatic perspective, Modupe Oduyoye

---

10. See Gordon Wenham, *Genesis 1 – 15: Word Biblical Commentary* (Milton Keynes: Word Publishing, 1991), p. 242.

says that Christianity inherited from the ancient Hebrews the conviction that the best kind of life was that of the nomadic herdsman. To be in the world but not of it, he writes, 'is to live like a Bororo among the Hausa or among the Bachana'. Such nomadic peoples, whether the Fulani in West Africa or the Masai in East Africa, need no exhortations to live as pilgrims; they do it all the time. Indeed, to witness a group like the Fulani breaking camp and moving on with their cattle as 'strangers and pilgrims' in the world in which the majority of people have made a permanent settlement is a salutary and challenging experience. As Oduyoye concludes, 'One cause of the conflict between Christian ideals and the reality of the lives of Christians is that in most parts of the world those who declare themselves Christians are by and large those who love the settled life.'[11]

Samuel Escobar has suggested that the subject of migration needs to become central to missiological reflection today and he records his own discovery of the manner in which, among Spanish migrants to France and Switzerland, the journey to faith in Jesus Christ was related again and again to 'the traumas brought to life by relocation'.[12] But if the phenomenon of migration in a globalizing world brings opportunities for Christian witness among displaced peoples, it also brings huge challenges to an old paradigm of mission according to which the fundamental movement in mission was from the West to the rest of the world. That pattern is now breaking up before our eyes as the movement of peoples around the globe brings large numbers of Christian believers from the Southern hemisphere into

---

11. Modupe Oduyoye, *The Sons of God and the Daughters of Men: An Afro-Asiatic Interpretation of Genesis 1–11* (New York: Orbis Books; Ibadan: Daystar Press, 1984), pp. 71–72.

12. Samuel Escobar, 'Migration: Avenue and Challenge to Mission', *Missiology* 31.1 (January 2003), p. 22. See the same author's book *A Time for Mission: The Challenge for Global Christianity* (Leicester: IVP, 2003), which brilliantly describes the present context of mission and contains illuminating examples of the theme of migration in mission.

the cities of Europe and North America. The faith of these peoples has not been shaped by the Enlightenment, with its rationalism and individualism, with the result that theologies and spiritualities originating outside the West offer searching challenges to traditional evangelicalism. How the churches of the West respond to this situation is a matter of crucial importance because, as Jan Jongeneel has said, 'Migrant Christians and their congregations and churches can help established Christianity in Europe to renew its mission and evangelism.'[13]

The danger inherent in settling becomes clear as the Babel story reveals the kind of ideology which now develops and underpins the activity of building a civilized and urban existence. Once again it is important to observe that what is being exposed and challenged here is not human cultural activity as such, since this can be understood as a genuine expression of our humanity, reflecting the fact that we are made 'in the image of God'. So, for example, Genesis 4: 17 describes the beginnings of human culture, including the building of a city, without criticism. Urbanization is not by definition evil, nor is the city beyond the scope of redemptive love. However, the problem with Babel is that this is a particular kind of project, designed to express human creativity and technological ability without reference to the Creator – or rather, in explicit rebellion against him. The builders here intend to create a city for themselves, with a glory that establishes 'a name for ourselves' (11:4). The elements of the story are, in Derek Kidner's words, 'timelessly characteristic of the spirit of the world' as the designers and builders 'betray their insecurity as they crowd together to preserve their identity and control their fortunes'.[14]

Now, I want to suggest that just as the perspective of Genesis 10

---

13. Jan A. B. Jongeneel, 'The Mission of Migrant Churches in Europe', *Missiology* 31.1 (January 2003), p. 33.

14. Derek Kidner, *Genesis: An Introduction and Commentary* (London: Tyndale Press, 1967), p. 109.

concerning God's gracious intentions with regard to the nations can be traced through the Bible, so also the contrasting message of Genesis 11 concerning human rebellion and arrogance forms part of the continuously unfolding story in both the Old and New Testaments. When the prophets turn their attention to Babylon, they see through the external splendour of the architecture and the undeniable skills of the builders to the God-rejecting and reality-suppressing ideology that underpins all this activity and propels it forward. Isaiah can acknowledge that the city of Babylon has a certain 'glory' (Is. 13:19), but it will be destroyed precisely because it represents and symbolizes the rejection of the living God: 'You said in your heart, "I will ascend to heaven; I will raise my throne above the stars of God . . . I will make myself like the Most High"' (Is. 14:13–14). In similar vein, but with yet more chilling words, Jeremiah declares: '"Even if Babylon reaches the sky and fortifies her lofty stronghold, I will send destroyers against her," declares the LORD' (Jer. 51:53).

In the New Testament, John of Patmos picks up this theme and recognizes the spirit of Babel at work in the Roman empire of his day. Like Babylon before it, Rome boasted of its achievements as though they represented the 'end of history' and absurdly imagined that it would last forever: 'In her heart she boasts, "I sit as queen; I am not a widow, and I will never mourn"' (Rev. 18:7). The chapter from which this statement comes describes in great detail the extraordinary trading networks of the empire which spread as far as China and India and literally sucked the wealth of the world into the city of Rome. Even today, two thousand years later, one can feel a sense of awe at the achievements of the Romans, but even as John describes the 'glory' of Rome he announces that it stands under judgment on account of its idolatry and injustice and he summons the people of God to 'Come out of her' (18:4).

Before we consider the implications of all this for mission today, there is one more aspect of the Babel story we need to notice. This narrative is quite clearly polemical in character. It is not merely an amusing folk tale intended to cause a smile but has a quite specific purpose to challenge the mythology and religion which provided the foundation for the kind of activity that is being described. It is well known that Old Testament scholars have discovered very many links between Genesis 1 – 11 and the epic stories told within the religions of the Ancient Near East. This means, of course, that these narratives originated within a religiously plural context and are quite explicitly responding to the issues which arise in such a setting. We might even say that the Bible at this point frequently speaks the language of the Babylonians and employs their idioms and concepts, while at the same time challenging and subverting the fundamental claims made in the pagan myths. The Babel story is the clearest example of this because, as Gordon Wenham points out, in this narrative the biblical authors throw discretion to the wind in an open and undisguised assault on Babylonian pretensions. He describes Genesis 11 as 'a spoof on oriental beliefs about the Mecca of Mesopotamia, the Esagil'. According to the myths, the temple of Marduk had been built by lesser gods with specially prepared bricks and its enormous height reflected the intention to reach up into heaven itself. Genesis, Wenham says, 'unmercifully batters these claims':

> It was, first, only a human building, and who would choose brick in preference to good Palestinian stone? And as for its vaunted height, so far short of heaven did this so-called skyscraper fall that God could hardly see it; he had to come down to look at it![15]

How then might this relate to the task of mission today? It is obvious that there are multiple lessons here. They include, for example, the obvious fact that there are fundamental principles of missionary communication across cultures embedded within the first chapters of the Bible. We do not have to wait for the appearance of the apostle Paul to discover that the revelation of God is capable of being translated and communicated in powerful ways in different

15. Wenham, *Genesis 1 – 15*, pp. 244–245.

cultures, or that such translation demands great gifts and strong faith. Engaging with the mythologies of Mesopotamia, entering into that very different religious world, and even employing its concepts in order to affirm the unique truth concerning the Creator God was a risky enterprise. But it was done, and done brilliantly, because the Bible is from its first pages a missionary book.

Consider for a moment what such an act of missionary communication actually meant for an individual involved in it. I referred earlier to the extraordinary story of the conversion of Nebuchadnezzar recorded in Daniel 4. Having been thrown into utter confusion by a dream that has terrified him, the king summons Daniel who he says, 'is called Belteshazzar, after the name of my god, and the spirit of the holy gods is in him' (Dan. 4:8). This sounds pretty alarming and it is not the kind of description one would want to be reported back to a mission home council! But is there in truth a finer example of missionary engagement in an alien cultural setting in the whole of Scripture? Daniel is absolutely in the world, but yet he is equally clearly not of it. Was this a key factor in the king's conversion, the presence of this man and his colleagues, so faithful, reliable and transparently honest, while all the time confessing the God who judges the proud and exalts the humble?

Our question concerning the relevance of this narrative to mission today can now be narrowed down by asking: what might be involved for us in imitating the example of the author of Genesis by bearing witness to our covenant God through the exposure of the falsehoods contained in the myths that lie at the foundation of our civilization? For many Christians in Europe and the United States this might seem an alarming and unnecessary question since they continue to assume that their culture remains basically Christian. They might also assume that talk about myths in the context of the modern world is misplaced since science and education have surely taken us above and beyond such primitive notions? On the contrary, I suggest that human beings continue to live on the basis of certain fundamental myths which are, as always, so much taken for granted that they are simply not recognized as what they are. Indeed, in our world of highly advanced technology, the need to recognize and examine such myths critically in the light of God's revelation is an urgent missiological priority because, as Claus Westermann says, the story of Babel 'anticipates the possibility of a development that would be realized only in the technical age in a way that would affect the whole of humanity'.[16] If we are really to hear and respond to the voices of Christians in the Southern hemisphere, like that of Ajith Fernando cited earlier, then we must be willing to reflect honestly and critically on the fundamental values that are shaping the world today and, in so far as these are discovered to be in conflict with God's will, they need to be challenged and subverted by a church as committed to mission in the modern world as the ancient Hebrews were in Mesopotamia.

My present post involves the development of a postgraduate course in the study of urban mission so I have been attempting to update my understanding of urban theory and analysis over the past few months. One of the books I have been reading is James Howard Kunstler's *The City in Mind: Notes on the Urban Condition* and it has been an unnerving experience to work through this while also reflecting at length on the biblical story of the Tower of Babel. Frankly, it is simply impossible to miss the parallels between the frenzied development of the modern cities Kunstler describes and the activity of those ancient builders at Babel. Now as then, there seems to be something driven, almost demonic, about the growth of a city like Atlanta, Georgia, where 500 acres of land in the metro region are bulldozed every week for new suburban development and 190,000 acres of trees were lost in a ten-year period from 1988 to 1998.[17] Kunstler describes his reaction on standing before the immense structure of the consumerist temple that is the Mall of Georgia:

16. Westermann, *Genesis 1 – 11*, p. 554.

17. James Howard Kunstler, *The City in Mind: Notes on the Urban Condition* (New York: The Free Press, 2001), p. 51.

One sensed, gaping at the immense 'landscraper' – as Leon Krier has termed these horizontal megastructures – that they could never, ever sell enough scented bath oil . . . out of the place to justify its existence, even over the relatively short depreciation period of the buildings (after which, for all anyone cared, the place might be sold for use as a for-profit prison or as the world's biggest evangelical roller rink).[18]

Surely in the light of this, our mission, like that of ancient Israel, must become polemical – the secular myths concerning money and possessions, false notions about what constitutes 'progress', the myth of redemptive violence which so saturates the media, and ideas concerning the nature of human identity and purpose – all of these must be exposed and challenged in the name of the living God who calls us to live within limits, to care for his world and for each other, and to recognize that we belong to a single human family within which all peoples are alike the objects of his loving concern and grace.

Called to be pilgrims

We return now to the text with which this chapter began: the call to Abram to depart from Haran and to go to an unknown destination with the promise that this action would set in motion a process leading to the blessing of 'all peoples'. Let me recall the connections between this initiative and Genesis 10 and 11 by quoting Johannes Blauw:

> The arbitrariness and overweening pride of the nations (Gen.11) prevents them from seeing reality, namely, that they have Yahweh to thank for their existence (Gen.10); therefore He will make them see reality by creating space in their midst for a nation (Gen.12) that is his special possession, in order to create space for his recognition among the nations.[19]

---

18. Ibid., p. 48.
19. Blauw, *The Missionary Nature of the Church*, p. 38.

In this final section, I want briefly to notice the significance of
Abram's departure from his country, his people, and his father's
household (12:1), but my main concern is to look at what happens
subsequently as he wanders as a nomad, or a pilgrim, among the
people of Canaan. The divine call to depart from his familiar and
loved home can be understood in two possible ways. On the one
hand, it can be seen as an absolutely radical move, especially given
the traditions of patriarchal life and the crucial importance of the
extended family. Some commentators focus on this aspect, suggesting that to move away from one's ancestral home in this way was
unthinkable in the ancient world. And, indeed, the three levels of sacrifice implied here, each one demanding more than the last –
'country, people, father's household' – seem to point in this direction,
indicating a break that was extremely demanding. What is more, as
we have already seen, the call to leave clearly stands in contrast to the
natural human inclination to settle which is so evident at the beginning of the previous chapter (11:1). So it seems clear that Abram's
action was counter-cultural and that it involved a movement that
created tension and conflict.

At the same time, the broader context provided by chapters 10 and
11 has shown us very clearly that migratory movements were occurring throughout the known world at this time. The Babel story ends
with people 'scattered over the face of the whole earth' (11:4), while
chapter 10 gives a precise description of these migrations which
result in 'the nations spread out over the earth after the flood' (10:32).
Seen in this context, Abram's move was neither unique nor particularly radical; he was actually part of a massive movement of peoples
across the world at a time when whole populations were on the
move. Theologically, what distinguishes his journey from those of
other people is that he makes it in response to an explicit call from
God. Other people are moving for a variety of social and economic
reasons; this man leaves home 'as the Lord had told him' and for the
sake of the kingdom of God. This prompts the question whether
today, in the age of globalization when thousands of people move
around the world motivated by quests that are often entirely secular,

Western Christians can still hear the voice that asks them to leave country, people and family for entirely different reasons and with a God-given vision of what this world can become?

The narrative in Genesis 12 contains an obvious and rather bleak contrast between the excitement and hope evident in the opening verses and sheer mundane 'ordinariness' of the long march that follows. The great promise given to the patriarch is related to a theophany – a direct revelation from God which was evidently so life-transforming in its glory and power as to open up a new dimension of reality. We have no detailed information about this, but it seems fair to assume that this was a 'night of glory' similar to a later theophany given to Jacob, when a barren landscape was suddenly transformed into 'the house of God' and 'the gate of heaven' (28:17). But then compare this with what follows: Abram, we are told, took his wife and nephew, and 'all the possessions they had accumulated and the people they had acquired in Haran' (12:5). The night of glory gives way to many days that are very ordinary, shaped by the usual concerns about possessions and people. Worse still, the 'Canaanites were then in the land' and for weeks, months, and years there were no visible signs that the promise received in Haran would come to fulfilment. Indeed, by the time of Abraham's death 'at a good old age, an old man full of years', the only thing he owns in this 'promised land' is the cave within which his bones are laid to rest (25:8–11). Surely there were times when he asked himself whether it had all been a delusion? Had God really spoken to him? Could so much have been staked on a vision that might turn out to be pure fantasy?

Notice though that the theophany in Haran seems to have been followed by other visitations in which faith was renewed and hope was restored. Genesis 12 reports that the patriarch erected a series of altars that dotted the landscape and marked those places at which the doorway between earth and heaven swung open and the pilgrim was reminded of what was really real. The first of these is at Shechem at 'the great tree of Moreh' where 'the LORD appeared to Abram and said "To your offspring I will give this land"' (12:6–7). There is another altar at Bethel, to which he returns at a later date, and the following chapters mention other occasions when God visits the patriarchs in a special way.

This seems to me to describe very well the life of faith: a life based on experiences of God and his grace which cannot be denied and result in a transformed view of the world and everything in it. We find something similar at the other end of the Bible where John of Patmos, imprisoned by an imperial power that seems to rule the world unchallenged and makes the confession that 'Jesus is Lord' seem rather hollow, finds himself 'in the Spirit' on the Lord's Day and catches sight of the reality of God in a way that relativizes all merely political claims and creates an alternative consciousness. We might say, therefore, that the Bible from beginning to end bears witness to the fundamental importance of a missionary spirituality. It seems to me that one of the challenges resulting from the great surge of Pentecostalism around the world involves the reminder that mission depends upon such knowledge. God must be something more than a 'language event' and without some occasions when, amid the gloom of this world, we see 'a door standing open in heaven' (Revelation 4:1), then faith will surely wilt and either degenerate into spiritless repetition or die altogether.

Let me emphasize the fact that we are not necessarily speaking here about conventional 'religious' experience. There is nothing predictable or routine about the appearances of the Lord to the patriarchs; they often come unsought and in contexts that are anything but 'religious'. Consider, for example, Abraham's encounter with Abimelech in Genesis 20. This is interesting because it involves an encounter with a representative of 'the nations' and serves as a reminder that, while God has now begun to work through a chosen people, he is still present and active in the wider world. At a point at which Abraham has actually lost his way and is placing the promise of God in danger, it is Abimelech who reproves him and points out his inconsistency. This leads the patriarch to confess that he had mistakenly assumed that 'there is surely no fear of God in this place' (20:11). This statement is later echoed by Jacob after another totally unexpected 'night of glory' beneath the stars when, having seen the door into heaven opened, he confesses 'Surely the LORD is in this place, and I was not aware of it' (28:16). This suggests that theophanies cannot be fitted into formulas found in spiritual how-to manuals, because God remains free and sovereign and works through surprising people and in unexpected ways. As the hymn-writer William Cowper put it:

> Sometime a light surprises
> The Christian while he sings:
> It is the Lord who rises
> With healing in his wings.

What is important is that, whatever the circumstances in which such encounters with the living God take place, we do know such altar-raising experiences. Some years ago my wife and I read a book of devotional readings written by a Christian Reformed theologian named Andrew Kuyvenhoven. I have misplaced the book but I wrote down this comment on Genesis 12:

> The life that is lived for God remains a mystery to the outsider. Every other life is lived from degree to promotion to paycheck. People measure their journeys by the houses they live in . . . But the life of the man of God is measured from altar to altar.

There is a final observation to make on this before we draw to a conclusion. If what has been said is true and we must know times of divine visitation, it also important to recognize that there are gaps between the altars. You can plot the places at which Abram built these altars on the map of ancient Palestine and they look rather like a diagram indicating the camps set up by mountaineers as they ascend some great peak. The point here is that in this life no one can live all the time in the exalted state that results from such nights of glory and, in fact, there may be very long days and nights on the pathway from one altar to the next. If the altars speak of the special presence of God, can we say that on the pathway between, during the many 'ordinary' days, there is sometimes a feeling of the absence of God? And if so, how do we cope with those days, or weeks, or even years?

Above all else, I suggest, we need to be honest about this. The temptation is to deny such 'absences' and to simply go on singing songs that tell of an experience we know to be remote from our day-to-day lives. The liturgies (if that is the correct term) and hymnologies of the evangelical world are notorious in their lack of a language that expresses pain and failure as well as joy and success. How often in a service of worship, struggling 'between the altars' and wearied along the way, do we find that the well-nigh exclusive concentration on celebration in worship compels us either to remain silent or to give expression to something we know to be a lie? The problem becomes even more acute when we move beyond a simple spiritual dryness, to the debilitating experience of suffering that induces serious questioning and doubt. The truth is that the Bible is replete with language that enables us to be honest in the presence of God about these things because, as the Old Testament scholar Robert Davidson put it, the song writers of ancient Israel discovered that the questions, 'Why?' and, 'How long?' were just as valid as the shout 'Hallelujah!'[20]

Let me conclude by applying this to the situation facing Christian missions at the present time. It seems incontestable that we are living through a period of major change and transition when very many received assumptions concerning the nature and practice of mission are being challenged. The change results from both the context within which Christians find themselves in the Western world – one which led the late Lesslie Newbigin to argue that the supreme missionary challenge of this, or any other age, was the conversion of the West – and from the emergence of world Christianity in Africa, Asia and Latin America. The voices we hear coming from those continents are often challenging, sometimes disturbing, and increasingly angry. Here, for example, is a well known preacher from West Africa:

---

20. Robert Davidson, *The Courage to Doubt: Exploring an Old Testament Theme* (London, SCM Press, 1983).

Gone are the days when all Africa would just sit down and organise one big crusade for one white man to come and turn all our pastors into ushers and counselors; the days when we would pack our bibles and go to a conference somewhere and listen to a white man lecture us on how to win Africa when he had not been to Africa before are over! *God is saying stand aside Ahimaaz.* You did it yesterday but today, stand aside because there is a new hour, a new day and a new man must deliver the message. *This is our time to reach our own.*[21]

It is not surprising if, in this time of change and uncertainty, Western Christians concerned to ensure faithfulness to Christ's irrevocable summons to mission, feel as though they are 'between the altars'. However, like Abram in such a situation, we are called to walk by faith and not by sight and to remember that the growth of the kingdom is actually a divine gift and that, while we are called to bear witness to the reality of God's reign through Christ, the Lord himself continues to work in the world, building that kingdom in ways that defy human analysis and perception. We need the reminder that the historical path that leads to the desired and prayed-for end sometimes passes through dark and gloomy valleys and trackless wastelands. As we have seen in chapter 3, a biblical theology of mission, as well as the study of the history of mission, leads to the conclusion that the wilderness belongs to God as much as does the well-watered garden and there are times when his purpose requires that the church goes through the former rather than the latter. What is needed, as Abram so clearly shows us, is faith in the final triumph of God and a reverent agnosticism as to precisely how, in a fallen and confused world, the desired goal will be reached. What is beyond doubt is that the ancient promise of blessing to the nations will be fulfilled, and in our own times we seem to be closer to the appearance of the church as a multinational fellowship than ever before in human history.

---

21. Mensah Otabil, *Beyond the Rivers of Ethiopia: A Biblical Revelation on God's Purpose for the Black Race* (Accra: Altar International, 1992), p. 81.

I want to end by listening to a voice from the Southern hemisphere which we heard earlier in this book, that of Kosuke Koyama. In a moving account of his own conversion in 1945, he describes how as a boy of 15, he experienced the carpet bombing of Japan in a night, not of glory, but of sheer terror. And yet, miraculously, in the morning the glory appeared:

> In the morning . . . I saw the sun rise as usual. As though nothing had happened in the human world. The light and warmth of the sun embraced both the dead and the living. The sun quietly erased the distinction between enemy and friend. I became aware that a strange quietness had descended on me. I heard, or felt, the words of Jesus, that God 'makes his sun to rise on the evil and the good, and sends rain on the righteous and the unrighteous'. Those words have come back to me from time to time for nearly sixty years since that morning. When I was baptized during the war, the minister told me that God loves everyone, Americans as well as Japanese. I was baptized, not into the religion of the enemy country *but into the God of all nations.*[22]

---

22. Kosuke Koyama, 'Reformation in Global Context: The Disturbing Spaciousness of Jesus Christ', *Currents in Theology and Mission* 30.2 (April 2003), pp. 119–120 (emphasis mine).